The Forgotten Vice-Commandant

Patrick Mc Sweeney is a registered Architect, Accredited Conservation Architect and Building Surveyor. He holds a master's degree in Building Conservation and is a partner in his own architectural practice in Limerick.

He has a keen interest in history which is not only confined to the Irish revolutionary period. His broad historical appetite also includes our built heritage, the history of architecture and art. Mc Sweeney's historical interest is also reflected in his professional architectural activities, where he has gained significant expertise specialising in the conservation of historic buildings.

A proud Limerickman born and raised in the city, his hometown's rich historical and often overlooked background has always inspired Pat, and the endearing connections his late grandfather shared with the city eventually combined and blossomed into the book he pens today.

Pat is a keen cyclist, which he actively pursues in his free time and is a member of Limerick Cycling Club.

The author can be contacted by email theforgottenvc@gmail.com

The Forgotten Vice-Commandant

A Grandson's Account of Johnny Mc Sweeney
Vice-Commandant of the 2nd Battalion
Mid-Limerick Brigade, IRA

PATRICK MC SWEENEY

Copyright © Pat McSweeney 2021
978-1-914225-38-3

All intellectual property rights including copyright, design right and publishing rights rest with the author. No part of this book may be copied, reproduced, stored or transmitted in any way including any written, electronic, recording, or photocopying without written permission of the author. Although every precaution has been taken to verify the accuracy of the information contained herein, the author and publisher assume no responsibility for any errors or omissions. The rights for images used remain with the originator. Permission for use of all images for the book cover and within this publication.
Published in Ireland by Orla Kelly Publishing.

Front cover photographs. Top image courtesy of Limerick Museum. Main photo courtesy of Eileen McNamara and Michelle Mac Sweeney.
Rear cover photograph: Courtesy of the George Imbusch photo archive. Colourising commissioned by the author.

To my dad; this is your dad!

CONTENTS

Acknowledgements	ix
Introduction	xi
Timeline of events	xiii
1. Early Years	1
2. Early Activities	7
3. Formation of the Irish Volunteers in Limerick City	17
4. Events leading up to the Rising of 1916	33
5. Aftermath of the Rising and before the War of Independence	46
6. Activities during the War of Independence	53
7. Internment in Wormwood Scrubs	60
8. Internment in Ballykinlar	72
9. The Civil War	91
10. The Republican Plot	106
11. Family life	126
List of references	134
Bibliography	145
Appendix 1 (Short account of what became of Johnny's siblings)	146
Index	148

ACKNOWLEDGEMENTS

Many people have provided invaluable guidance and generosity throughout my research. I would particularly like to thank Thomas Toomey, author of the magnificent book *The War of Independence in Limerick*, for his help, expert insight, and encouragement to publish this book. Similarly, Des Long for his encouragement, oral history, insight into all things republican, photographs, and access to his vast personal library (you'd have to see it to believe it).

Joe Kenny, a reservoir of family information, whose contributions, interest, and encouragement were much appreciated. Br. Terry Mac Sweeney—Johnny's nephew and the sole living relative of my father's generation, for his oral accounts, old documents, photographs, and proofreading. Conor Boyle from Donegal who generously provided the hut photograph of Ballykinlar, which I was so grateful to obtain. Coincidentally, Conor is currently writing a book about his grandfather, who was interned in the same hut as Johnny in Ballykinlar.

I am grateful to Dr Conor Reidy for his help with copy editing and Dr Ruan O'Donnell for his helpful suggestions, Eileen McNamara for her assistance in reviewing old documents and photographs, together with Michelle Mac Sweeney, who allowed me to access and use family photos. I am particularly grateful to Mary Ryan for pictures of her grandfather's Ballykinlar autograph book, Maurice Quinlivan TD for making available to me the minute book of the Limerick Republican Graves Committee, and Frank and Niall Imbusch for allowing me to use their father's unique panoramic photographs taken during the Civil War period.

Many thanks to my work colleague Miroslaw Malinowski for his expert help with graphics, Paul Doyle for proofreading, and Patricia Rogers for her interest, encouragement, and eye for reviewing old photographs.

I am also grateful to the staff at the national and local archival institutions and Libraries for their assistance.

My special thanks to the following:
- Michael King of the County Down Museum and Ballykinlar History Hut who was extremely helpful to me.
- Brian Hodkinson (now retired) and Dr Matthew Potter in the Limerick Museum
- Sean Cafferkey, Jean Turner, and Anna-Maria Hajba at the Special Collections and Archives, Glucksman Library, University of Limerick
- Hugh, Noelle, and Linda at The Military Archives Bureau of Military History, National Library
- Aoife Torpey at Kilmainham Jail Museum/OPW
- Clare County Library and Archives

INTRODUCTION

From my earliest childhood memories, I recall my father frequently taking me to visit my grandfather's grave in the Republican Plot in Mount Saint Lawrence Cemetery, Limerick. He told me stories about how my grandfather had been a member of the old IRA who fought for Irish independence and how he died in prison due to these activities.

My grandmother, who lived with us, used to show me the mementoes she had of her husband: his service medal, which she kept in a drawer in her bedroom dresser, the harp he made in Ballykinlar Internment Camp—which she proudly displayed, and the picture of him upon his release from Wormwood Scrubs Prison.

Although I was exposed to these close relatives who were alive during this turbulent yet momentous and fascinating period in Irish history, I had no structured knowledge of the details of any roles my grandfather undertook during the 1916 Rising, the War of Independence, and the Civil War. This lack of awareness appears to have been a common occurrence amongst all his grandchildren. This was apart from the odd stories we heard, some of which may well be true while others were likely embellished over the years. Despite that, I always felt that he played a central role, which deserved to be uncovered and recorded. Fascinated by the mythology surrounding the man and the period and motivated by the curiosity that my father and grandmother instilled in me at an early age, I set out to produce a simple research document primarily for my family's benefit.

In 2011, I began my quest to address these inconsistencies by requesting and researching my grandfather's pension records.

These documents initially confused me, and I was somewhat demoralised as they posed more questions than they answered. They confirmed he died in Limerick City Home; I was always told he died in prison. That he was captured in Buttevant; what was he doing in Buttevant? Why was my grandmother refused a pension if he had active service, and why did his medal not have a Comrac bar if he had seen active service?

As I drilled into these records, I began to uncover numerous revealing avenues of research. Piece by piece, I started to unravel my grandfather's story, my document gradually taking on a life of its own. After years of engrossing research, my findings morphed into a book that was far beyond my original intention. It is the culmination of all the information I have gathered and provides insight into the life and events of my grandfather in a chronological and fully referenced manner. In addition to highlighting and preserving his story for prosperity, I trust that this book will pay modest tribute to a man who gave himself unselfishly in the fight for Irish freedom and to whom I am proud to be related. I hope this publication will also highlight Limerick's understated role in the national struggle for independence.

In recounting my grandfather's activities, I felt it was essential to provide context, and I have highlighted and explained the story of the Irish struggle for independence in parallel. I have done so in a simple manner that makes no assumptions about the reader's knowledge of the history of this period.

TIMELINE OF EVENTS

The Fenian Movement/ IRB – 1858 to early 1900s
Attempts to establish Irish independence from Britain are not just early 20th-century events. Numerous nationalist movements attempted various rebellions and counter-revolutions in Ireland over the centuries of British occupation. The most recent prior to the 20th century was the Fenian Movement. Formed in 1858 as the Irish Republican Brotherhood (IRB) it was a highly secretive political organisation dedicated to the establishment by force of an independent Irish Republic. Its members became known as Fenians and were active not only in Ireland but also in Britain and the United States. Whilst their various campaigns in the late 1800s did not secure freedom for Ireland, it did however establish a spirit of Irish rebellion which carried into the 20th century and inspired the men and women to take part in the series of events that ultimately led to Irish independence.

Formation of the Irish Volunteers - 25 November 1913.
The Irish Volunteers was a nationalist military organisation initially set up as a direct response to the perceived threat of the - then recently established - Ulster Volunteers, a unionist militia strongly committed to remaining part of the United Kingdom with a stated purpose to resist Home Rule by force if necessary. As events unfolded, the Irish Volunteers went on to become the IRA (Irish Republican Army).

Easter Rising - Monday 24 April 1916.
This was an armed insurrection staged during Easter Week 1916 that lasted six days. The Rising was mounted by Irish republicans with the aims of ending British rule in Ireland and establishing an independent Irish Republic. While the Rising failed militarily and led to the execution of sixteen of its leaders (fourteen in

Kilmainham Jail, one in England and one in Cork) who became martyrs, it did, however, succeed in galvanising widespread Irish public support and a desire for independence.

War of Independence - commenced 21 January 1919, a ceasefire was agreed 11 July 1921.

This was a guerrilla war by the IRA against the superior military machine of the British army, which led to Ireland's independence. Although a truce began on 11 July 1921, hostilities only formally ceased with the signing of the Treaty on 6 December 1921, which granted independence to a twenty-six county Ireland that was to remain in the British Commonwealth and required its TDs to swear allegiance to the king.

The Civil War - commenced 28 June 1922 and ended 24 May 1923.

This bitter war between former comrades who fought for independence was caused as a result of deep divisions created between pro-Treaty and anti-Treaty supporters. Those who favoured acceptance argued that the powers it granted made it worthy of support. They believed it would ultimately lead to an Irish republic by accepting the principle that while it did not achieve the ultimate freedom that all nations desire, it would give them the freedom to achieve it and the only alternative was renewed war with Britain. The Treaty's opponents criticised it mostly because of the requirement of elected deputies in Dáil Éireann having to swear allegiance to the king and its failure to achieve the status of a republic for a thirty-two county Ireland. In effect, they saw it as a desertion of the Republic they had sworn to defend since it was proclaimed in 1916 and ratified by the first elected Dáil in 1919, thereby confining the country to dominion status within the British Commonwealth.

CHAPTER 1

EARLY YEARS

My grandfather John (or Johnny as he was known), was born in 1881 and was the oldest son of six children (1). His family home during his early years was 5 Benson's Lane, Limerick. This lane, long since gone, ran adjacent to, and intersected Mungret Street across the road from the Market House (see map on page 5). Both of his parents were from strong Fenian families and this tradition was no doubt instilled in Johnny from an early age. His father, Denis, a brush maker, was born in Cork circa 1850 and resided in an area known as Sober Lane in the city. He then moved to Dublin for a period before finally settling in Limerick (2). He died in August 1904. His mother, Catherine Hogan, a housewife, was born in Limerick and was the same age as her husband, she died in January 1912. Johnny had two brothers, Denis and Patrick, and was six and nine years their elder respectively. He had three sisters, Mary Ellen, six years his elder, and Annie and Katie, who were one and three years younger respectively.

Both parents and all their children appear to have had some education, as they were listed in the census of 1901 and 1911 as being able to read and write (3). Patrick (or Paddy as he was known), the youngest at the time of the 1901 census, was aged eleven and was still at school. He was the only one of the family who listed Irish and English as his languages. It is somewhat surprising that, in the 1911 census, neither Johnny then thirty, nor any of his siblings, indicated an ability to speak Irish, despite their interest in the Gaelic revival. The two younger sisters worked as tailoresses while the oldest worked as a machinist. Johnny and his two younger brothers were employed as brush-makers. As the photograph on the next page indicates, all three worked in the family brush-making business located in Market House, 44 Mungret Street, Limerick.

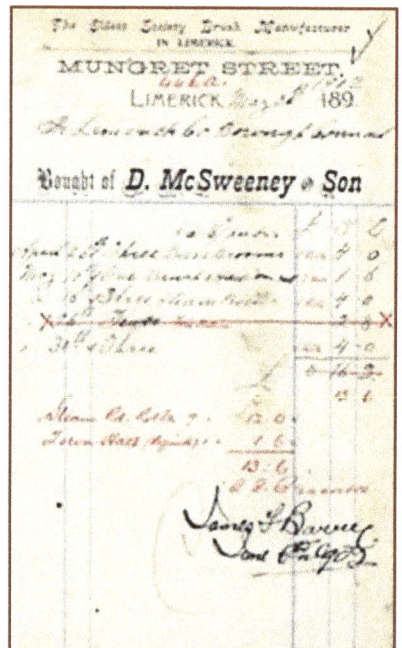 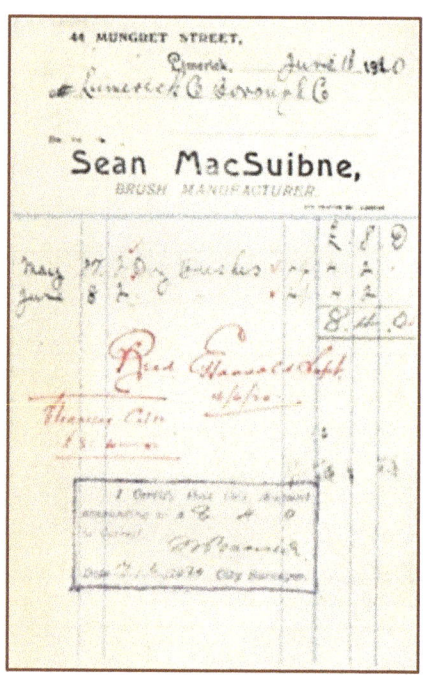

Bill heads issued to Limerick Corporation. The document on the left is dated 1902 contained Denis's name (Johnny's father). On a later bill dated 1910 the name changed to Seán and was translated to Irish. *(Courtesy Limerick Museum)*

Johnny, in what was his second marriage, married my grandmother, Catherine (Kate) Walsh, on the 28 April 1913. Kate

Early Years

This photograph, circa 1910 (4), shows (from left), in aprons, Johnny and his two brothers, Denis and Patrick. The non-aproned elderly man is an unrelated delivery man known as a carter (5). The photo is taken outside the Market House on Mungret Street, which still stands today following substantial refurbishment in 1995. It is now a protected structure or listed building (6). Their father's name (Denis) 'D. Mc Sweeney Brush Manufacturer' is over the door. He was deceased at the time of the photograph (since 1904). Note also the brush heads stacked on the left.

(Family photograph-colourised by author)

was the daughter of a civil servant (Telegraphs Inspector) and the oldest daughter of nine children (7). They had six children (five boys and one girl) (8).

Michael, J.	born	4	July	1913
Denis, Gerard	born	14	Oct.	1914
John, Joseph (Roger- my father)	born	28	April	1916
Patrick (Pearse)	born	13	April	1918
Robert (Bertie)	born	3	April	1920
Mary Rosaleen (Sister Mary or Sister Rosa)	born	20	March	1923

The family home was 33 Mungret Street (9). The ground floor of this three-storey premises was listed as a bakery on a map dated 1897 (see next page). The family may, therefore, have occupied the two overhead floors, and most likely resided at this address from the date of their marriage until circa 1928, when Kate, then a widow, moved with her young family to St. Patrick's Road, Limerick. This Mungret Street address should not be confused with the Market House (or 44 Mungret Street) on the same street from which the brush-making business operated.

I recall my father informing me as a child that his father had a son who died at the age of ten before he married Kate. The following documentary evidence confirms this memory. Johnny, at the age of twenty, did not reside in his parents' house at the time of the 1901 census. Ten years later, at the time of the 1911 census, he did reside in the house. This was two years before his marriage to Kate (10). A marriage record exists that a John Mc Sweeney married a Mary Nagle of the Sand Mall on 15 July 1900 (11). The census of 1901 recorded that Johnny, then aged twenty-two, lived in 44 Mungret Street with his wife, Mary, and two in-laws. This was the same address as Market House where the brush-making business was located. They most likely resided on the first floor. Burial records reveal that his wife Mary was laid to rest on 31 August 1907,

Early Years

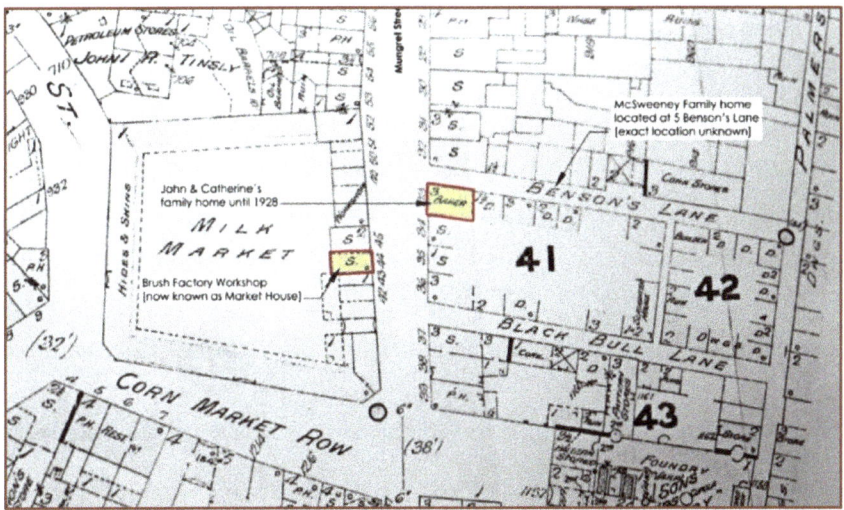

Insurance Plan of the Mungret Street area of Limerick dated March 1897 highlighting the various family homes and the brush manufacturing premises. The numbers written within each house indicate the number of floors and the letters 'S' or 'D' indicates shop or dwelling.   *(Courtesy Limerick Museum)*

Photograph (c. 1950s) of the lower two floors of the front and side of Johnny's marital home, 33 Mungret Street, Limerick. The lane to the side is Benson's Lane where he originally resided in his parent's family home. The brush-making business later moved from Market House to the single-storey outbuilding to the rear of this building.   *(Courtesy Terry Mac Sweeney- colourised by author)*

in what would appear to be a common plot used by the City Home, or Limerick Union as it was then known. Records also indicate that a boy named Joseph Mc Sweeney, aged four, of 44 Mungret Street was buried in December 1908 in the same family plot as Johnny's mother and father; there are no other burials recorded in this graveyard from this address. These records also indicate that this child was born in 1904. Be that as it may, I have found that the ages of persons given on burial records are often unreliable. Indeed, Johnny's burial records claim that he was thirty-eight when he died, when he was actually forty-two. This child, therefore, could well have been somewhat older than the stated four years but unlikely to have reached the age of ten as I had initially remembered.

CHAPTER 2

EARLY ACTIVITIES

Johnny had a great interest in and love for hurling and he played with the club of which he was a founding member, Young Irelands. In a *Limerick Leader* article, he was described as, 'a hurler of note'. The article noted that 'no man did more for Gaelic pastimes in Limerick than the late Comd. Sean Mc Sweeney' (1). He won two county medals in 1902 and 1910, playing corner-forward against Monagea and half-forward against Castleconnell in the respective finals (2). In the latter game, where he scored three points, he had a particularly good game as the match report in the *Limerick Leader* stated that 'Mc Sweeney was a host in himself and these points gained Young Ireland their victory.' He was also a member of the Young Irelands selection that beat Dublin 3-10 to 1-3 in the semi-final of the Croke Fennelly cup* in July 1909 only to be beaten by Thurles Blues (now Thurles Sarsfields) 1-11 to 1-7 in the final (3). Other great games with which Johnny was associated in Young Irelands included a victory over the Dublin Faughs in the Gaelic League Oireachtas final in Croke Park (or Jones Road as it was then known) in July 1911. He was also part of the defeat of Ballingarry in the John Daly Cup final at the Markets Field in February 1912 in which the noted veteran Fenian John Daly (see paragraph on John Daly in next chapter) threw in the ball (4).

*The Croke Fennelly Cup: In 1909, Archbishop Thomas Fennelly, who succeeded Archbishop Croke, donated the magnificent trophy to Archdeacon Innocent Ryan, pastor of Fethard, Co. Tipperary. He organised a hurling tournament for the trophy, now named the Croke/Fennelly Cup, with the aim of paying off a parochial debt. The tournament featured teams from eight counties and the Cup could be won outright by any club who won it three years in a row. This Thurles Sarsfields achieved in the years 1909, 1910, and 1911.

Young Irelands GAA Club was founded on 16 November 1898 as an offshoot of the Young Ireland Society. Johnny was listed as an attendee together with eight others at this inaugural meeting held in the headquarters of the Young Ireland Society in 55 Thomas St. Limerick (5). The original aim of this club was more to capture the youth and train them for a place in the ranks of the IRB (Irish Republican Brotherhood), rather than become a serious force in hurling ranks. This objective was made more difficult for those whose sole interest was hurling because recruits to the club were hand-picked and could only be admitted when it was certain that they fulfilled the conditions demanded by the political needs of the day (6). However, despite this, Young Irelands went on to become the strongest hurling club in Limerick until the emergence of Ahane in 1931. They were the glamour club of their day and attracted many players who moved into the city to work (7). They won seven county titles, which placed them sixth overall, right up to the present day in terms of club titles won. Their last title was won in 1932 (8).

Johnny also appears to have been a highly regarded and accomplished match official as his name frequently appeared in newspaper reports as a referee in important games. He refereed the 1912 County Senior Hurling Final in the Market's Field where

Fedamore triumphed over Ballingarry (9). According to the *Limerick Leader's* account, it would appear that he had his work cut out for him refereeing this important match. In a headline that read: 'UNSEEMLY SCENE AT COUNTY HURLING FINAL MATCH IN MARKET'S FIELD, MARRED BY DISGRACEFUL CONDUCT': the game resulted in the sending-off of three players, while another player was forced to retire due to injuries received in the aftermath of the altercations. The account went on to describe the serious and unprecedented incident that occurred ten minutes into the game following an altercation between two players that developed into fisticuffs.

> About 100 of the supporters of each team broke in over the railings. Some of the outsiders lashed hurleys and ashplants most unmercifully on the heads of players and spectators. The field was turned into a regular battleground, and the disgraceful scenes which lasted for about 20 minutes, surpassed in brutality and savagery the faction fights which took place in bygone days. It is difficult to imagine how any rational beings could behave towards each other as those who took part in yesterday's exhibition. It was indeed a miracle that there were not some lives lost. Several persons interested themselves as peacemakers, but the efforts were of no avail, as they were set upon by the howling mob, waylaid with hurleys and ashplants, and when knocked down were kicked on the ground. Blood was now flowing profusely and some bandaged heads were conspicuous. A spectator who was sitting on the wall of the county infirmary got so excited that he fell off the wall a height of about 20 feet and received a nasty wound on the head and had to be attended to by a priest. After some time a scene unparalleled in the history of Gaeldom in Limerick ended (10).

The article concluded that Johnny was a most impartial referee. He was also a member of the GAA County Board where it seems he was highly regarded. He served as treasurer of the board in 1909 where it is stated that 'he did trojan work with the result that the county finances after years in a bad state were at last put on a sound footing' (11). In addition, he also was elected vice-chairman in 1907 and often presided as chairman of the board when the need arose (12). From the various articles about the County Board meetings published in the *Limerick Leader* at the time, he came across as quite vocal. In one instance while being critical of the shortcomings of an individual appointed by the secretary, he demanded that the board as a body take overall responsibility for the appointment rather than laying the blame solely on the secretary (13). This was a sign perhaps, of his no-nonsense, pragmatic approach to decision-making which was to serve him well in his role as a senior military officer in later years. Articles in the *Limerick Leader* stated that Johnny through his love of hurling

> was all that a Gael should be, full of admiration for any scientific combination whether it was composed of Cork men, Tipperary men, Kilkenny or Limerick men. He saw beyond the game on the field and knew that such stalwarts would, when the call came, be eager to do the harder and nobler thing-fight for the land whose games they played." And that "because his career was typical of many at the time, it would serve as an illustration of how gaelic and Volunteer activities were intertwined. His sole outlook on life was the twin progress of games and nationality (14).

Johnny also served on the committee of the Limerick Guardians (who were responsible for the workhouse in the city) and in later years, served as vice-chairman of the organisation (15). He was also a leading member of the IRB (Irish Republican Brotherhood) in the city from an early age. Also, Johnny and his brother, Paddy, amongst others, were part of the early founding members of Na Fianna in Limerick. Both attended the first meeting in 1911 which

Early Activities

Photograph of the Young Ireland team that won the County Championship in 1910. Johnny is pictured seated far right on the middle row. See endnote (16) for full list of names.
(Family photograph)

was addressed by Bulmer Hobson, the Belfast man credited as being the brainchild behind the Fianna. Paddy, in particular, was quite involved at senior officer level in the Fianna. He was, according to his obituary in the *Limerick Leader* and witness statements, its first commandant taking charge in 1917. The reference 'first Commandant' most likely relates to a command restructuring that took place in 1915 [17]. He also received a service medal for his role in this grouping. Another founding member who played a central role in its organisation, who worked as a railway clerk in Limerick at this time, was Seán Heuston, who later took part in and was executed for his role in the 1916 Rising. Limerick man Con Colbert who was executed after the Rising, also assisted the formation of the Fianna in Limerick. In the early days, the Limerick Sluagh (branch) or the 'Sluagh Lord Edward Fitzgerald' as they were officially titled was also addressed by no less than three others executed following the 1916 Rising, Roger Casement, Tom Clarke and Sean Mc Dermott [18]. Patrick Pearse also visited and gave a lecture at the Fianna Hall [19]. So, I am sure the two brothers, through their association with the formation of the Fianna in the city and later the Volunteers, would have been very familiar with most, if not all, of these nationally well-known and regarded Republican figures. An account states that Johnny, 'for the Fianna boys he would go to any trouble. On them, he looked as the hope of the country, and to that end, he maintained his interest in the lads he was to term 'the best boys in Ireland' [20].

While in appearance Na Fianna was essentially a Boy Scout movement, in reality, however, it was much more than this. It was often described as the young wing of the IRA. The organisation was open to boys between eight and eighteen years of age. Pearse described Na Fianna's role as 'to train the boys of Ireland to fight Ireland's battle when they are men' [21].

Its militant character is obvious from the first three clauses of its constitution which stated:

> Object
>
> To re-establish the independence of Ireland by training the youth of Ireland.
>
> Means
>
> The training of the youth of Ireland, mentally and physically, to achieve this object by teaching, scouting and Military exercises, Irish history, and the Irish Language'.
>
> Declaration
>
> I promise to work for the independence of Ireland, never to join England's Armed Forces, and to obey my superior officers. (22)

A typical weekly session programme for a winter session of the Fianna was advertised in the *Limerick Leader* as follows;

> Monday-Physical culture; Tuesday- Squad and company drill; Thursday -Irish language and history; Friday; signalling and first aid. Competent teachers have been secured for all subjects, and valuable prizes would be offered for competition at the end of the session (23).

The importance placed on the learning of Irish culture and, in particular, the language is evident in an address by John Daly to the Fianna in May 1913.

> He asked them to remember that the mind be trained as well as muscle and urged them to endeavour to acquire a thorough knowledge of the history of Ireland, for unless they know the story of the country, they could never love her as they ought. Every member of the Fianna should also strive to obtain a good knowledge of the Irish language. What difference, he asked, was there between the majority of the Irish people and their tyrannical oppressors. He feared that judging by the language they spoke, there was none, for by their tongues they were all English. The older generation had found the country crushed to the earth

beneath the iron heel of England and had little or no opportunity of learning the native language, but the young men of today had opportunities in plenty and should avail of them. What a pleasure it would give him to pass down O'Connell Street and hear the Fianna converse in their own language. When Ireland spoke Irish the days of the British Government's term of office in this country would be numbered (24).

Photograph of a young Vincent Kenny, Johnny's Nephew (his sister Kate's Son) in Na Fianna uniform. *(Courtesy Limerick Museum-donated by Joe Kenny)*

Early Activities

Fianna Eireann boy scouts (1913). Photo taken outside Na Fianna headquarters at the back of John Daly's house on Barrington Street. Sean Heuston is seated in the centre holding walking stick. Vincent Kenny (Johnny's sister Kate's Son) is in the front row (the fourth from the right) wearing medals. This hall was later burnt to the ground by the Black and Tans in the War of Independence.
(Photograph- Courtesy Limerick Museum- donated by Joe Kenny)

The Forgotten Vice-Commandant

Na Fianna commanded huge respect and played a crucial part in the struggle for independence. They were hugely instrumental in the landing of arms from the Asgard in Howth in 1914. In the early years, they attended drilling and marshalling events. Later, during the War of Independence in April 1919 when martial law was introduced in Limerick and the city was a no-go area for adults, the Fianna ran errands for the Volunteers and this included relaying orders from GHQ (General Headquarters) in Dublin (25). They also provided guard duty on the ground floor entrance hall of the Volunteers headquarters in Transport Union Hall on O'Connell Street.

Display case containing medals obtained by Johnny's brother Paddy and his brother-in-law Fred Kenny (who was married to Johnny's sister Kate). From left Fred Kenny's War of Independence service medal, Paddy's Na Fianna service medal and Paddy's War of Independence service medal.

(Courtesy of Joe Kenny)

CHAPTER 3

FORMATION OF THE IRISH VOLUNTEERS IN LIMERICK CITY

In order to comprehend, in my opinion, the not insignificant role played by Johnny in the formation and operation of the Irish Volunteers in Limerick, along with his subsequent roles in the War of Independence and Civil War, it is necessary to have an understanding of events that were occurring in early twentieth-century Ireland.

After seven centuries of British occupation, there was a reawakening or renaissance in all things Irish sometimes referred to as the Gaelic revival or Celtic Dawn. Nationalism was at the forefront and nationalist organisations such as the Gaelic League and the GAA were formed in the late-nineteenth century. Home Rule or self-government for Ireland was actively lobbied for in the British House of Parliament by the Irish Parliamentary Party led by John Redmond. There was a real expectation, after two failed attempts in the late-nineteenth century, that Home Rule would finally be granted to Ireland by the British government. In 1912, however, the Ulster Volunteers were established. This grouping was effectively a unionist militia strongly committed to remaining part of the United Kingdom and whose stated purpose was to resist Home Rule, by force if necessary. To counteract this grouping, the nationalists formed a military organisation known as the Irish Volunteers in 1913, and its declared primary aim was 'to secure and maintain the rights and liberties common to the whole people of Ireland' (1). The Volunteers were formed primarily from two nationalist organisations, the Ancient Order of Hibernians (AOH) and Sinn Féin/IRB (2) (although there were others, including the Gaelic League and the Trades and Labour Council). The AOH was a nationalist collective committed to securing Home Rule by peaceful or political means and was closely linked with Redmond's Irish Parliamentary Party. This group had by far, of the two organisations, the more widespread popular support of nationalists throughout the country. Sinn Féin was the public face of, and secretly encompassed the IRB. The IRB was a highly secretive group and grew out of the Fenian movement which was founded in the 1850s. Although the Fenian organisation and the IRB were separate, the movement as a whole was known as Fenianism. The IRB's watchword was 'Soon or Never' and their uncompromising position was to overthrow the English government by force of arms and to establish an Irish Republic (3). It was the IRB that was behind the initiative which eventually led to the inauguration of the Irish Volunteers in November 1913 (4). Though the Volunteers' stated purpose was not the establishment of a republic, the IRB through their involvement intended to use the organisation to do just that. They recruited high-ranking members at national level into the organisation, notably Joseph Plunkett, Thomas MacDonagh, and Patrick Pearse, who was co-opted to the Supreme Council in 1915. These men, together with Thomas Clarke, Sean Mac Dermott,

Eamonn Ceannt and James Connolly of the Irish Citizen Army, constituted the Military committee, the sole planners of the 1916 Rising. The IRB was highly secretive and organised into circles. A 'circle' was the equivalent to a regiment, that the 'centre' or A, who might be considered equivalent to a colonel, who chose nine B's, or captains, who in their turn chose nine C's, or sergeants, who in their turn chose nine D's, who constituted the rank and file. In theory, an A should only be known to the Bs; a B, to his Cs: and a C, to his Ds; but this rule was often violated (5). The IRB secrecy is evident from the witness statement of War of Independence veteran Patrick Whelan (6) where he states that it was only when he was sworn into the IRB that he then realised that his own father was, in addition to being a member also, the then head-centre for Limerick city. Johnny was a member of the IRB from an early age (and its public face, the Wolfe Tone Club) and he was a head-centre for an IRB circle in the city (7). This would have been a very high-ranking and respected position, and he would have been reporting directly to the head centre for the city, who would, over the course of years, include distinguished Fenians in the city such as John Daly* and Seoirse Clancy*. Additional confirmation of his senior position in the IRB is evident in the book titled *Not While I Have Ammo*, where Johnny is documented as swearing in the subject of the book Captain Connie Mackey in 1917 'into the 4th division of the IRB, an honour offered to only the most dedicated of the volunteers' (8).

*Seoirse Clancy was an active Volunteer, who was executed by Crown forces while Mayor of Limerick in his home in 1921. He is pictured with Johnny and a number of other officers in the photograph on page 23 taken in Killonan in 1915.

*John Daly was a leading and highly-respected Republican figure in the Limerick area or 'old Fenian' as he was often named. A former mayor, he resided in 15 Barrington Street where there is a memorial plaque to his name/ family. The Fianna Hall mentioned earlier was located behind his house and the Volunteers often held meetings in his house. He died two months after the Rising in 1916 and the Limerick senior hurling county championship cup (the John Daly Cup) is named after him. His nephew Ned Daly was executed for his part in the 1916 Rising in Dublin for his role as commander of the Four Courts. His niece (Ned's older sister) Kathleen Daly was married to Tom Clarke, an Irish revolutionary leader, and the first signatory to the proclamation. He was arguably the person most responsible for the 1916 Easter Rising. Clarke who spent fifteen years in prison on explosive charges in England, was closely associated with John Daly as both of them were imprisoned together under very harsh conditions in penal servitude in Chatham prison. He worked for a while in Limerick and was a frequent visitor to the city while he was planning the rising and he frequently holidayed in Kilkee.

Following the establishment of the Irish Volunteers nationally in 1913, a conference and an initial meeting were held in Limerick city to organise a city branch of the Volunteers. At the first meeting of this group, which was held on 17 December 1913 [9], Johnny was co-opted onto the committee of the Volunteers in the city. As noted previously, at this time he was a member of the IRB [10] and as such would have been at the more Republican spectrum of the two main organisations involved in the setting up of this grouping. Following a number of initial meetings, an inaugural public meeting of the Volunteers was held on Sunday evening 5 January 1914. This was attended by two visitors from Dublin, who were to become, as events unfolded, nationally well recognised and respected Republican figures. Patrick Pearse, who was seen to be the embodiment of the later 1916 Easter Rising in Dublin, signatory to the proclamation and was one of the sixteen leaders executed for his role in the Rising (although at this time he was not a member of the IRB). Roger Casement (as I will outline in the next chapter) organised the shipment of arms on board the ship the *Aud* from Germany and was later hanged in London for his role in this shipment. In his address to the Limerick public meeting, Pearse emphasised the need for drilling and organising to ensure that they were able to meet what he referred to as 'circumstances that might imperil the chances of Home Rule'. Roger Casement also addressed the meeting and he drew comparisons to the manner in which the Boers in South Africa had stood up for their rights. Casement fought in the Boer War in the British army and stated that 'he had entered the war fighting for the greatest empire on the earth but ended it on the side of the Boers as he had developed a great admiration for the Boers on account of the manly way in which they had fought and died against great odds' (11). Michael O'Callaghan who was later to become Lord Mayor and who in turn would be executed in his home by Crown forces also spoke and advocated the merits of the points borne out by the previously mentioned figures.

Following the first initial meeting, it is noted in Toomey's book, *The War of Independence in Limerick* that John Daly received a letter from Casement who requested that they send copies of the *Limerick Leader* with reports of the meeting (12). In the letter, he also expressed a wish to visit Limerick again (which he did for the Volunteers first parade). Also, in a letter from Tom Clarke to John Daly, it was stated that both Pearse and Casement were unanimous in stating that the meeting at Limerick was the best in every respect of any such meeting they have attended. It is also noted in the same book (13) that Casement again wrote to Daly expressing a wish that he would look after a German journalist who was to come to Limerick and put him in the way of seeing 'the true nationalists of Limerick not the shoneens' (an Irishman who imitates English ways). Toomey also states that it is obvious from Casement's contact with a German journalist and his postings of a copy of the *Limerick Leader* abroad that he was involved in getting the message of the Irish Volunteers out to the world media. In February 1915, Pearse declared in Irish that 'there are many who think that the Limerick Battalion is the best we have. They are good men in good command; most of this loyalty, courage and determination are not surpassed

The Forgotten Vice-Commandant

in Ireland' (14). Both Casement's letters and Pearse's comments in my view are highly significant and pay enormous tribute to the Limerick City Volunteers of which Johnny no doubt played a large part through his role on the committee at the time of its founding, later as an officer and his high-ranking membership of the IRB. Further testament to this fact is also noted in the book *Limerick's Fighting Story*. Johnny's name is recalled amongst a number of men 'as being the pioneers of the early days of the Volunteers' and it is further stated, 'that due to the efforts and sacrifice of these men the Limerick City 2nd Battalion IRA became an active force in the fight for Irish freedom' (15). An additional testament to the input and influence Johnny no doubt had in the early days of the Volunteers in Limerick is evident from the fact that a further group march of the new Volunteer Corps led by two bands was arranged for St. Patrick's Day 1915. A large number of Volunteers, said to be 700 started out from Johnny's business premises the Market House in Mungret Street and was reviewed by Roger Casement, who came from Dublin especially for the event (16).

The following is an account from the witness statement of IRB member Joseph Barrett who was from County Clare which gives a

OPPOSITE
This family photograph shows Johnny last on the right back row. It was also published in Thomas Toomey's book *The War of Independence in Limerick* which he titled 'a group of prominent Volunteers taken in Killonan in 1915' and named them as follows: L to R (REAR) James Leddin, Honorary Battalion Colonel*, Robert Monteith (who later accompanied Roger Casement to Germany and arrived on Board the *Aud* in Tralee Bay- see also chapter 4), Rafe Slattery 2nd Lieutenant*, Tom Pigott & Johnny Mc Sweeney* L to R (FRONT) Seoirse Clancy (later to become Mayor of Limerick and head centre of the IRB in Limerick and murdered in his home by Crown forces), Mick Corbett, James*Connaughton and Phonsie Kivlehan. * denotes names and/or ranks in 1916 which I have inserted which were left blank in the above-mentioned book (17).

(Family photograph- colourised by Stephen O'Doherty)

Formation of the Irish Volunteers in Limerick

good insight into the influence that the IRB had in the formation of the Volunteers;

> Limerick City was the Divisional Centre (of the IRB) for Munster. Meetings of this Divisional Centre were held about every six months in Limerick City. I attended most, if not all, of the meetings of the Munster Council as one of the I.R.B. representatives from Clare. The general trend of the discussions at these meetings, however, was that the Council wanted to ensure that the I.R.B. was in control of the Irish Volunteer organisation because, through such control, it would be in a position to handle any situation that might arise. This objective, to a great extent, was successfully accomplished. I do not remember many of the other people present at these Munster Council meetings, as they were mostly strangers to me at the time. I do recall having seen there Michael P. Colivet, Jim Leddin, - Dundon, all from Limerick City; Seán Hegarty, Cork, Pakie Ryan, Doon, Art O'Donnell, Sean McNamara, Con Kearney and Ned Fennell, all from County Clare. At one of the Munster Council meetings in Limerick held, as far as I can remember, between May and September 1915, it was made known to the men present that a Rising was contemplated at some future date. As far as I remember, but I am not quite sure, I think it was Seán O'Hegarty from Cork that made this statement. That statement was expected by many of the men present and did not appear to create much surprise (18).

No doubt Johnny through his role as a head centre for a circle in the city would also have attended these divisional centre meetings and as such would have known at a very early stage the plans for the Rising. I also suspect it was through his senior role in the IRB in the city that Johnny was co-opted onto the organising committee of the

OPPOSITE
On Parade in Laffin's field, Killonan in 1915. Johnny is pictured third from the left. To his immediate right is his brother-in-law Fred Kenny, who was married to his sister Kate. Fred Kenny died in June 1920 after he took ill some nights after being shot in the groin during an attack on a Barracks (19).
(Photograph Courtesy Limerick Museum- donated by Joe Kenny- colourisation commissioned by author)

Formation of the Irish Volunteers in Limerick

Volunteers. In order to assist with the above-stated ambition of the IRB, i.e. to be 'in control of the Irish Volunteer organisation because, through such control, it would be in a position to handle any situation that might arise'.

Structure of the Volunteers in Limerick

In the early days of the Volunteers, up to approximately early 1917, the Limerick Brigade, which covered a large portion of the midwest area, was commanded by M.P. Colivet. The Brigade had eight battalions, one in the city, three in the county (of which one included a portion of Tipperary) and four in County Clare [20]. However, this organisation's hierarchy changed sometime after the Rising, as I will outline later. The Limerick City Battalion was originally known as the 1st Battalion but it experienced a split in December 1916 largely caused by the view that officers were reluctant to fight and particularly had issues with their role in the Rising [21]. A new battalion known as the 2nd Battalion was formed. Not only was Johnny highly instrumental in the formation and setting up of this new battalion [22], an account states that the coming into being of this battalion can be attributed to him in a very large measure [23]. Ernest Blythe, the Volunteer organiser who was tasked with setting up and drilling battalions throughout the country and who went on to become the first Minister of Finance in the new government also confirms Johnny's role in setting up the new battalion in his witness statement as follows.

> After a lot of talk with Peadar MacMahon, Peadar Dunne and three or four Limerick people, including Johnny Sweeney and Martin Barry, we decided that it would be impossible to stir those in charge of the existing Volunteer body in Limerick to action. We then agreed that the only thing to do was to organise a second battalion and we set about doing it [24].

Formation of the Irish Volunteers in Limerick

A group of Volunteers in Laffin's field, Killonan in 1915, Johnny is pictured eighth from left on the back row. Robert Monteith is pictured on the right front row.
(*Courtesy of Mercier Archives*)

An account also suggests that Johnny was quite friendly with Ernest Blythe, and that he used to stay at his house on occasion when in Limerick (25). Blyth also spoke highly of the Limerick Brigade when he recalled that 'Limerick was the best' in an RTE television interview in 1965 about his experiences in setting up and organising the Volunteers throughout the country (26).

Following the setting up of the new battalion, the 1st Battalion continued on in name but was mostly defunct until later in the War of Independence when the two battalions joined up again but continued on in name as the 2nd Battalion. This new unit was made up of five companies A, B, C, D and E. These companies were formed based on hurling club locations within the city. For example, the Treaty club on the Thomond side of the city-sponsored A-Company, St Patrick's and Claughaun clubs sponsored B-Company (27). Johnny was part of and, became captain of B-Company before being promoted to Vice-Commandant of the 2nd Battalion (28). This battalion and the largely defunct 1st Battalion were two of five battalions of a brigade known as the Mid-Limerick Brigade, the other three consisting of;

The 3rd Battalion made up of Castleconnell and Murroe.
The 4th Battalion made up of Caherconlish and Fedamore.
The 5th Battalion from Patrickswell and Adare (29).

All these battalions reported to the Mid-Limerick Brigade, who in turn reported directly to general headquarters in Dublin. The remainder of Limerick County was divided into two other separate brigades known as the West Limerick and East Limerick Brigades. The latter turned out to be a particularly formidable fighting brigade. A new brigade was also set up to cover the county of Clare.

From an article in the *Limerick Leader* (30), it would appear that the credit for the following methods of obtaining guns for the Volunteer

Formation of the Irish Volunteers in Limerick

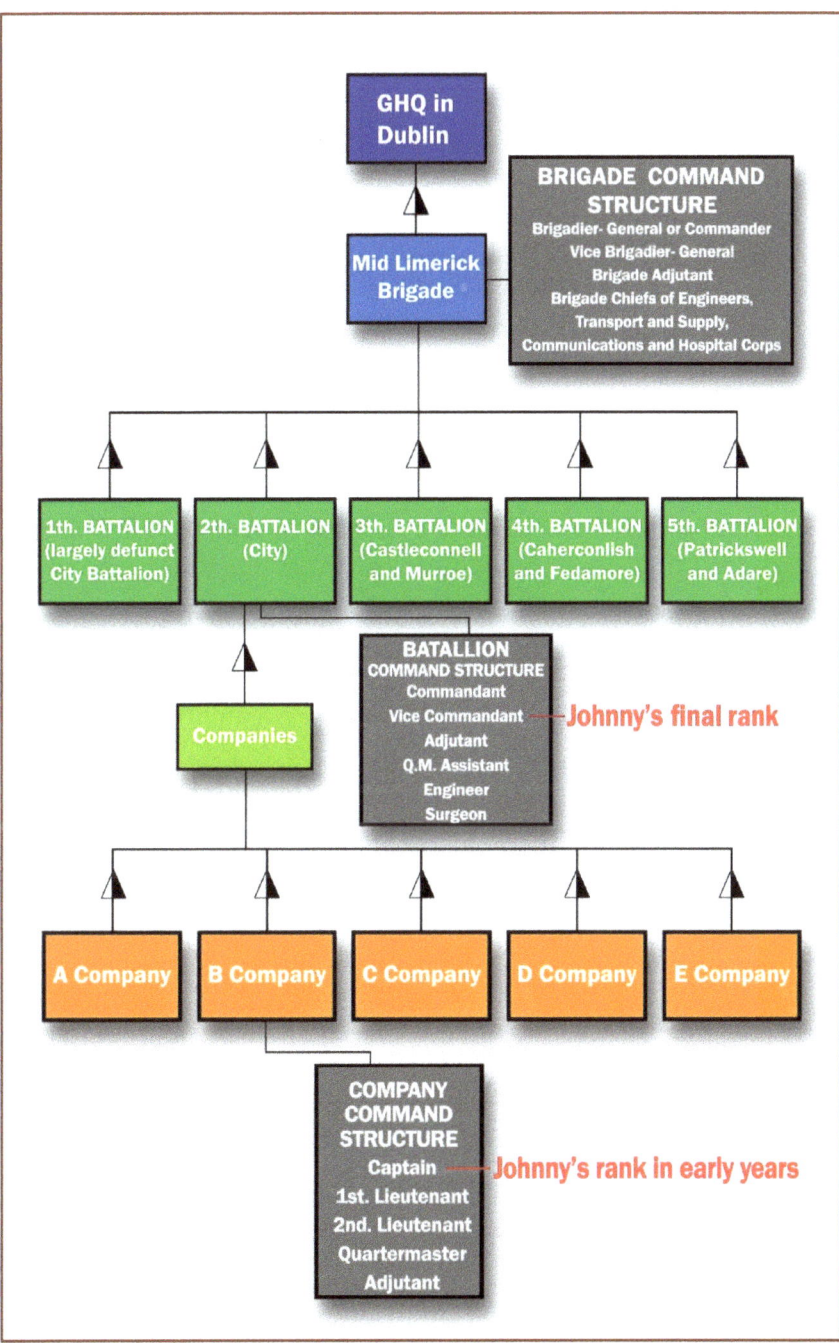

Diagram indicating the structure of command of the Mid-Limerick Brigade during the War of Independence period and Johnny's rank (32).

(Diagram by author)

movement in the early years as described by Jeremiah Cronin in his witness statement can be attributed to Johnny.

> Some soldiers of the garrison were got at and were induced to steal them from the barracks. As these could not be brought out the barrack gate direct, other means had to be found. After some planning, an idea took root. A small four-wheeled trolley was made to which was attached a long length of rope sash line used for hanging sashes and placed in a convenient place inside the barrack railing on the military roadside where there is a disused quarry (known as the Widow Fitzgibbons) and away from the public gaze. The rifle was strapped on to the trolley and, at a given signal, was hauled out through the bars, and so another rifle was added. The soldier was well paid and everyone was happy (31).

In addition to the IRB and Na Fianna, another important cog in the Republican movement was Cumann na mBan which was formed in 1914 as an organisation for women who would work in conjunction with the Irish Volunteers. Members assisted the Volunteers by gathering intelligence, transporting and hiding arms, nursing wounded men, providing safe houses and organising support assistance for IRA men in prison. Some women also took an active military role as was the case with Constance Markievicz where during the Rising she was appointed second in command to Michael Mallin in St Stephen's Green. They played a particularly important role in both the 1916 Rising and the War of Independence.

> **OPPOSITE**
> Illustration showing the Limerick City Battalion Volunteers uniform in 1915. Note the hat that the Volunteer is wearing is known as a Cronje hat worn for 'fieldwork', Johnny is pictured wearing this hat in the photograph in chapter 3. Missing from the illustration are the regulation pointed cuffs that Johnny is also wearing in the above-mentioned picture. The gun shown is an M1898 Mauser Rifle of the type landed at Howth in 1914 and distributed around the country.

Formation of the Irish Volunteers in Limerick

Legend: 1. Cap badge designed for the Limerick Regiment, **2.** Belt buckle, **3.** Brass tunic button, **4.** Brass shoulder badge, **5.** Peaked Cap. **6.** Pocket size rosary beads and leather pouch, **7.** Regulation haversack containing a mug (a), mess tin (b), knife, fork and spoon (c), spare shirt (d), spare socks and a towel and soap (e).
(Artwork by Artist from the book Irish Volunteers 1913- 1923 copyright Osprey Publishing, part of Bloomsbury)

The Forgotten Vice-Commandant

A group of Volunteers parading in Laffin's field, Killonan in 1915
(Courtesy Limerick Museum)

In Limerick Madge Daly, John Daly's niece was the president of the provisional committee of Cumann na mBan from its inception until after the Civil War in the city, with the exception of one year, and was the driving force of the branch.

It has been suggested that Johnny's wife, Kate, was an active member, but I have found no evidence in the organisation's membership records to confirm this. However, in her pension application files, there is a letter written by Dan Burke TD in 1951 in support of an application by Kate for an increase in her pension that states that she was a member of Cumann na mBan. The likelyhood is that this may have been somewhat an embellishment of the truth by the TD as she never herself, in all her numerous correspondence and appeals, mentioned that she was a member. Records do exist however that Johnny's sister in law (his brother Paddy's wife) Rebecca (nee Moloney) was an active member (33). Her Limerick Volunteer cap badge is pictured on the cover of this book.

CHAPTER 4

EVENTS LEADING UP TO THE RISING OF 1916

In the lead up to 1916 the Limerick City Battalion was sent a welcome addition from general headquarters in Dublin, a man by the name of Captain Robert Monteith who was described as follows in the witness statement of James A. Gubbins (1);

> A welcome accession of strength had arrived in the person of Capt. Robert Monteith. He had served in the British Army and had been active in the Volunteers in Dublin, so active that he had been served with an order requiring him to leave that city. He took charge of training and soon put things humming. Company parades were held on several nights a week. Officers classes were formed, the lessons of which were put to the test during the Sunday route. A note in the "Irish Volunteer" about this time remarked "The Limerick Regiment has struck a recent visitor from Headquarters as perhaps the most efficient in Ireland. In some respects it leads Dublin.

Johnny is pictured with Monteith and a number of other senior officers in Killonan in 1915 (see photograph in the previous chapter). The Volunteers used to drill in a field on a farm owned by a Mr Batt Laffin in Killonan (in the vicinity of the premises currently in use as a Nursing Home which was originally the farmhouse). Shortly after this picture was taken Monteith disappeared in August 1915 and an account stated;

> Towards the end of August 1915, the men discovered that Monteith was gone - to Kilkenny, it was said. No hint had been allowed to reach them of his intention to leave and they regretted his departure deeply. During his nine months stay he had performed trojan work and his personality and his ability had won their genuine regard. His destination was Germany via the U.S.A. His return to his native land was by way of Banna Strand on Good Friday 1916 (2).

This paragraph had much significance as I will highlight. The stated plan for Limerick's role in the Easter Rising at this time, according to several accounts (3), was that a German ship known as the *Aud* was to arrive in Tralee Bay from Germany on Good Friday laden with rifles, a number of machine guns with personnel to man them, and ammunition. Roger Casement and the above-mentioned Monteith who had secretly left Limerick to assist Casement with securing arms in Germany, were to accompany the *Aud* in a German submarine. It is interesting to note that in an early plan (just two months before the Rising), Limerick was considered as the chosen location for the landing of the arms. Because of the city's location on a tidal estuary and the fact that it could depend on a high level of support from the well-trained local Volunteer Regiment. However, German strategists eventually decided against Limerick, choosing the wide-open beach in Ballyheigue instead. Upon the arrival of these arms, the plan was that the Kerry battalion would deliver the arms to Abbeyfeale. The Limerick Brigade was to march to this location and take whatever arms were required and deliver the surplus via train to Galway in a rendezvous in Crusheen (approximately ten miles north of Ennis). Once armed, the stated intention for the planned insurrection was to hold the Limerick/Killaloe line and also Limerick City if possible. The British forces based in the city at that time consisted of 800 infantry, a battery of artillery and about 100 constabularies. As the most the Limerick Brigade could hope to muster would be about 200 armed men, the plan was to hold the north shore of the Shannon in the city, including the bridges, with the intention of retiring into Clare should the necessity arise. The Castleconnell Battalion was to man the Limerick/Killaloe line and conform to the movements of the City Battalion. The Galtee Battalion was to make the Galtee mountains the base of its operations. Meanwhile, the West-Limerick Battalion would fight on its own ground while the Clare men formed a base for the City Battalion. This action was planned to commence at 7 pm on Easter Sunday (4).

At the parade on Holy Thursday night, the commander of the Limerick Brigade, Michael Colivet, having received the above formal instruction on the Tuesday of that week, gave his instructions for the planned Easter Sunday's mobilisation. The battalion was to march to Killonan for exercises which would continue on Monday. Every available man would parade, carrying arms and ammunition and two days rations. Any man unable to parade should hand over his rifle to his Company Officer. He strongly encouraged those present to exert themselves to mobilise every available man. He instructed the battalion officers to remain behind after the dismissal and to them he gave the details of the planned insurrection. It was not entirely unexpected, as the IRB members of the battalion, of which Johnny was a member, had known for some time what was going on and hints had reached the battalion officers (5).

Then began the bitter sequence of disasters. On Good Friday. two Limerick men, Tommy Mc Inerney and Sam Windrim, were detailed to take cars to Killarney (6). They were due to reach there at 8 p.m. to pick up five men (three of whom were wireless operators) arriving by rail from Dublin. Michael Collins in GHQ had charged them with the responsibility of making contact with the *Aud* and to convey them to Cahirciveen (7). They contacted their men, three of whom, including Con Keating, and a wireless expert, sat in the second car. During the night drive, Tommy Mc Inerney lost sight of the tail light of the first car, missed the turn and plunged over the pier into the estuary at Ballykissane. The three passengers were drowned but Mc Inerney escaped only to be arrested later (8).

Meanwhile, the *Aud* arrived in Tralee Bay at the agreed time, but her signals went unanswered as, apparently due to the above-mentioned car accident and the drowning of the signalmen, two green signal lights were never erected at the designated landing place as had been planned (9). The captain of the *Aud*, a man named Spindler, decided to spend the night hiding behind Ilauntannig Island (one of the Magharee Islands) in Tralee Bay. At dawn, they were approached by a British ship and while initially, they managed to bluff that vessel into thinking they were a Norwegian cargo ship, later on, the same day, Good Friday, the *Aud* was arrested. While under escort to Cork, the crew of the *Aud* sank the ship (with all the guns and munitions still on board), identified themselves as sailors of the German Navy and surrendered (10).

Meanwhile, Casement and Monteith had earlier (in the early hours of Good Friday morning) landed on board the German submarine in Banna Strand, Co. Kerry. Casement was arrested but Monteith managed to escape and made his way to Ardfert six miles outside Tralee (11).

Events Leading up to the Rising of 1916

Images of Roger Casement and Capt. Robert Monteith with German officers on board a U-boat leaving Germany the afternoon before they landed at Banna Strand. Casement is pictured in the centre with a moustache. His beard was shaved off to avoid recognition. Second, from the left is Monteith also with a moustache. To the right of Monteith is a man called Bailey who also accompanied them to Germany. *(Courtesy of Mercier Archive)*

A colleague of Johnny's in the 2nd Battalion, Pat Whelan (who were later to be arrested together and interned in Wormwood Scrubs), was dispatched from Limerick to find out what was going on in Kerry. He managed to make contact with Monteith in Tralee – who had made his way there from Ardfert – and his witness statement details an account of their conversation.

> He (Casement) stated that the Germans wanted cheap Irish blood and were interested only in so far as the Irish caused some diversion or upset the English war machine at the time. He also said that the rifles which were aboard the sunken boat were not of much use and that they were rifles which had been captured off the Russians. There were no machine guns or men to man such.

He told me to tell Colivet (the Commander of the Mid-Limerick Brigade) when I got back to Limerick to bluff his way through as best he could. He also stated that the Germans had an extraordinary idea of the position in Ireland and were under the impression that if about a dozen machine guns were placed in strategic positions in Ireland, we would be able to sweep the British out of Ireland (12).

Pat Whelan arrived back in Limerick on Easter Monday morning and immediately travelled to Killonan where he informed the officers in charge of the situation with the *Aud*. However, it would appear that the officers were already aware of the facts, as on Easter Sunday morning orders were received from the leader of the Volunteers in Dublin, Eoin McNeill, cancelling all the orders for the Rising nationally largely as a result of the sinking. Although the plans for the Rising were cancelled it was decided to proceed with the mobilisation and a parade of the City Battalion in Killonan was organised whereby about 140 men attended and over 110 stayed overnight on Monday (13). Johnny was at Killonan but was suffering from appendicitis that Easter weekend (14) and an account stated that;

> Johnny was in a very delicate state of health, so delicate that he was ordered by his doctor to go into hospital for a serious operation. Instead of doing so, he worked feverishly that week to ensure that every man in a section would be in his place when they hoped for fight began. Off he went rifle on the shoulder, gay and the gayest, and at all times he was in agony. Never a word of complaint, lest he would be ordered home, which he undoubtedly would have been if the officer commanding was made aware of his ailment. Never did a more loyal or fearless soldier take the field in the defence of his country's honour (15).

Shortly after Whelan arrived Ms Agnes Daly (John Daly's niece) arrived in Killonan with a dispatch which read; 'We started at noon today, carry out your orders. Signed P.H. Pearse' (16). This countermanding order caused complete confusion as the Limerick Command were unsure Pearse was aware of the sinking of the *Aud* and they wondered if there was another ship on some other part of the coast. The reality was that none of the insurrections planned could be carried out in the absence of the expected arms. There were fewer than 150 rifles in the City Battalion, and the outside units were poorly equipped. Each Volunteer was served with fifty rounds of ammunition and marched back to Limerick. The Volunteers assumed they would be fighting that evening but when they arrived

McNeill's Orders cancelling the Rising published in the Sunday Independent on Easter Sunday, April 23, 1916. Together with reports of the incidents in County Kerry, the significance of these separately reported events were unknown at the time of publication.

back in Limerick they were told to 'stand to arms' in their homes and await further instruction.

A meeting was held the next day, Tuesday 25 April, consisting of all the officers, battalion staff, company commanders and all the officers who had any knowledge of the previous events which Johnny attended. After some discussion, it was decided by a majority of ten to six not to proceed with any insurrection. Johnny was one of the six who voted to proceed with the Rising. Captains Liam Ford, Michael Brennan from Clare, Major James Mc Inerney, John Lane and Seán Ó'Murthuile (a member of the Supreme Council of the IRB) also voted to fight (17). In addition to voting for insurrection at these meetings Michael Brennan, in his pension application, further recalled that both he and Johnny amongst others including Seán Ó'Muirthuile and Tom McInerney (possibly should have said James) attempted unsuccessfully to persuade the Limerick Volunteer leadership to either fight or give their arms to those wanting to fight (18).

The following is Michael Brennan's witness statement account of this meeting:

> The Limerick Provisional Committee met that evening and we debated for hours whether or not we would obey this instruction. The whole controversy turned on who was entitled to give the orders – Mac Neill or Pearse. Only six of us were in favour of fighting and our case was that our comrades were already fighting in Dublin and our duty was clear, no matter who gave the orders. We had about 25 against us and the meeting got heated and unpleasant, but the minority were in a hopeless position as all the senior officers and officials were against us. Most of Tuesday was spent in conferences and meetings at which feelings became more and more bitter, but nobody on either side altered his views. It was arranged to meet again on Wednesday, but it was clear that no decision to fight would be taken by this committee, so I decided I would go to Galway and contact Mellows who was "out" with the men. I arranged with my friends in Limerick that if I found the

> Rising had actually started in Galway I would come back to Limerick and report. We would then collect all men willing to fight and all the arms on which could lay our hands and move to Galway picking up my Clare men en-route (19).

As events unfolded, Brennan was unable to get to Galway as he was met and turned back on every road by armed RIC (Police) patrols. It became obvious to him that there was no prospect of getting to Galway except by force. He decided to return to Limerick and collect a party strong enough to overcome any opposition they would meet on the way. Given his noted willingness to fight irrespective of the local leadership's views, Johnny would no doubt have jumped at the chance to join Brennan in his endeavours. However, it was not to be, as Brennan was arrested at a roadblock on Sarsfield Street on his return to Limerick and imprisoned in Limerick Jail before being sent to Frongoch Internment Camp. Brennan in his witness statement gives the following interesting account of this arrest (20).

> I was taken into the Shannon Rowing Club beside the bridge and put into a tiny room with a soldier who had his bayonet fixed and who remained all the time at the "engage" position with his knees bent and the point of the bayonet about a foot from my chest. At first, I made fun of him, but he was mute, and I realised after a while that he was so nervous he was actually dangerous, so I also remained silent. After about an hour I was removed under a heavy escort to William St.R.I.C. Barracks and from there to Limerick Prison.

While it is clear that Johnny, by virtue of his attendance at this meeting, was an officer at this time. However, it is not clear what his exact rank was. He was referred to as a section-commander and a member of what was known as the civil committee (21) and separately referred to as a member of the management committee.

In addition, as he was also quite significantly, IRB centre for a circle in the city (22). Given that the IRB were the main instigators of the Rising, I would be of the view that he was never going to vote against the direct countermanding order of Pearse who was a member of the IRB, whereas McNeill who issued the original order was not. I suspect Pearse would have known this and that is why he issued the countermanding order in the hope that IRB members throughout the country would be able to convince brigade commanders to ignore McNeill's orders and proceed with the planned insurrection. A positive vote at this meeting would have resulted in almost all of the Mid-West Region rising, as the Limerick, Clare and part of the Tipperary Brigades, who at that time were under the control of the Limerick Brigade, were awaiting the decision of this meeting as to whether the planned insurrection would occur (23). As it turned out, because of this vote the Limerick Brigade was not to join the only other areas where the Rising took place outside of Dublin which were in Carnmore in Galway, Clarenbridge, Enniscorthy in Wexford and Ashbourne in Meath. Instead, this meeting, which resulted in the subsequent surrender of arms, appears to have sowed the seed of discontent which bitterly divided the City Battalion and led to the setting up of the 2nd Battalion in early 1917, which Johnny was very instrumental in setting up.

An account of the events of Easter 1916 in Limerick states in its conclusion that 'they [the Limerick Brigade] were ready and willing to do their part, and if they did not go into action, the fault was not theirs' (24). This statement may well hold true collectively for the Limerick Brigade because of the series of disastrous events that occurred. However, this statement serves to highlight how committed and determined Johnny and five of his comrades were to take part in the Rising. As being fully aware of the overwhelming odds against them and mindful that they would not be criticised for not taking part, they still nonetheless not only voted for but strongly argued in favour of proceeding with the planned insurrection.

While the above-noted plan for the Easter Rising in Limerick appeared doomed due to the sinking of the *Aud*, Jeremiah Cronin in his witness statement gives an interesting insight into what the Volunteers felt what the new plan was to be:

> When Easter Monday dawned, there were intense feelings of suspense, nobody knowing what was going to happen. A little way from the main body, the officers were grouped together in a very earnest debate. What the new position was we did not know. No doubt the plan of campaign was being worked out. All we knew was outside Volunteers were to come into Limerick and seize the General Post Office one body from Meelick under Michael Brennan, and another from Castleconnell under Sean O'Carroll. I understand the march of the Mid-Limerick Brigade, as we were known, was only a move to throw off the suspicion of the authorities. It was made to look like an ordinary Sunday parade (25).

While this may first appear somewhat at odds with the stated plan to hold the north bank of the River Shannon, it perhaps gives an insight into the utter confusion and speculation that existed. Or maybe some credence can be taken from this statement that there may well have been a plan to stage a local uprising knowing that the intended plan for a national uprising lay in tatters following the sinking of the *Aud*.

Following the events of Easter 1916, Monteith at this time must have been one of the most wanted men in the country. He surely would have faced execution had he been captured and indeed he stated as much in his autobiography (26). He made his way back to Limerick where he hid out in Batt Laffin's house in Killonan. He remained in hiding there for six months sleeping in a dugout on the farm at night for fear of arrest, before he made his way to the USA disguised as a priest (27). A niece of Johnny's, Angela Kenny, recalled to her nephew Joe Kenny that her older siblings (both of whom were in the Fianna – one of them Vincent is pictured in Fianna uniform in Chapter 2) used to cycle to Killonan with parcels of food for two men hiding out there in a dugout.

There is an interesting footnote to this chapter on the Easter Rising. From my research, it would appear that Johnny would have known (or at least met with) no less than nine of the sixteen executed leaders of the Easter Rising in Dublin and possibly more, given his IRB connections. These nine leaders, which would have also included four of the seven signatories to the proclamation, were Patrick Pearse and Roger Casement (on at least three occasions) from the early days of the Volunteers and Na Fianna. He would have been familiar with Seán Heuston from the formation of the Fianna in Limerick and, by association Limerick man Con Colbert who also was heavily involved with Na Fianna and frequently visited Limerick to assist with its foundation. Also, it would not be conjecture to assume (given his strong IRB connections) that, John Daly's nephew, Limerick man Ned Daly, would have been well known to him. Again by association, so would Ned Daly's brother-in-law, Tom Clarke. Clarke also resided in Limerick for a while (circa 1913) was also involved in Na Fianna at this time. He was a frequent visitor to John Daly's house after he moved to Dublin (28). It is highly probable, that he also met – if he had not already done so – Sean Mc Dermott, a close friend of Clarke and a senior IRB figure who also frequently visited Limerick. He would also have had an earlier opportunity to meet Mc Dermott as he also addressed the Limerick Fianna earlier in 1913 and the City Volunteers in August 1914 (29). He likely encountered Thomas Mc Donagh and Willie Pearse (30) during their visit to Limerick in 1915 for the Whit Sunday parade, something that was essentially a fundraiser for the Limerick Volunteers which attracted countrywide attendance. Following the parade, these men amongst many others, including Pearse, Ned Daly, Tom Clarke and, although not part of the Rising, Terence McSwiney – who later died on hunger strike – all visited John Daly's house where they were introduced to prominent local IRB members (31). All of these nine, with the exception of Casement, who was hanged in London, were executed by firing squad in Kilmainham Jail shortly after the Rising.

CHAPTER 5

AFTERMATH OF THE RISING AND BEFORE THE WAR OF INDEPENDENCE

In the days immediately after the Rising the British administration in Ireland's panicked reaction was to round up known republicans and general dissidents not only in Dublin but from all over the country. Most of those arrested were detained and screened in Richmond Barracks in Dublin before being transferred via prisons in England and Scotland to a detention camp in Frongoch in north Wales.

While wholesale arrests had been made in Dublin, and throughout the south and west of Ireland no such arrests were initially made in Limerick. The man commanding the British forces in Limerick City, Anthony Weldon, who was thought to be a fair and reasonable man, did nothing initially beyond parading three regiments of infantry and an artillery brigade, together with a regiment of cavalry, as a mild sort of threat. However, his hand was forced by headquarters in Dublin and about fifty Limerick City Regiment and County corps were arrested (accounts differ somewhat) and detained in the Mid-Limerick Brigade area [1]. Most were released shortly afterwards (2). One account suggests, that it was because of the surrender of arms in Limerick, which was negotiated with Weldon through the then Bishop of Limerick Thomas O'Dwyer, that the British Commander decided that no arrests would take place in Limerick city or county following the Rising (3). This surrender of arms bitterly divided the City Battalion.

From my research, there is some evidence to suggest that Johnny and his brother, Paddy, may also have been arrested and sent to Mainland Britain and interned in Frongoch Internment Camp in Wales. This evidence includes primary sources such as his newspaper obituaries in two national newspapers, *The Freemans Journal* and *The Irish Examiner* (4). Both of these stated that Johnny was interned in Frongoch after the Rising and also the former newspaper reported that he spent another period in prison in 1918. Also, a *Limerick Leader* article states that Paddy was one of the first to be arrested after the 1916 Rising (5). Primary sources are an oral account from Johnny's nephew, Brother Terry Mac Sweeney (who is Paddy's son) whose recollection was that both men were indeed interned in Frongoch. In addition, he recalled that Paddy was sent to Wandsworth prison before being sent to Frongoch. Further but inconclusive proof, is a manuscript held in Clare County Museum prepared by Art O'Donnell from Co. Clare while he was interned in Frongoch. It contains Johnny's name and address handwritten on a page (6). Art O'Donnell was later to be interned with Johnny in Ballykinlar. However, this source is somewhat inconclusive in that while initially I thought that it may have been an autograph book, it turns out on closer examination from the handwriting, that it was most likely an address book. Notwithstanding this, while the possibility may exist that both Johnny and Paddy may have been detained initially after the Rising, I have been unable to obtain conclusive evidence to confirm that either were interned in

Frongoch and it is, therefore, highly likely that they were not. All evidence seems to suggest that no Limerick city-based Volunteers were sent to Frongoch save for Tommy Mc Inerney, who, as mentioned earlier, was the driver of the car that went off the pier in Kerry on Good Friday. Also, it would appear that from the official lists of detainees in Frongoch (7) that any other Volunteers with a Limerick city address were interned as they had taken part in the Rising in Dublin. Notwithstanding this, although again unconfirmed, there is also the possibility that Paddy and Johnny may have been sent only to Wandsworth Jail in England and returned back to Ireland without been sent to Frongoch as was the case with a number of the prisoners initially detained. A notable example was Limerick man Sam Windram, the driver of the other car involved in the accident in Kerry on Good Friday, where an account suggests that he was released from Wakefield Prison (8). Although there are other more credible conflicting accounts that Windram was actually sent to Frongoch.

However, it is important to understand the significance that this detention camp had in the future events as they unfolded. Frongoch Camp was at that time a recently vacated internment camp used to house German prisoners of war. It was a former whisky distillery that had closed at the outbreak of the First World War and consisted of two camps titled the North and South Camp. An account states that:

> If the execution of the leaders of the Rising was a major mistake by the British in their reaction to the rebellion, the second major mistake was Frongoch. Here were housed nearly 1900 of the finest of their generation and became a veritable political university and military Academy….it became a fertile seeding ground for the spreading of the revolutionary gospel…. aptly described as a 'university for revolutionists' or "Sinn Féin University"(9). It was described in Al Neeson's life and death of Michael Collins that "Frongoch, Reading

jail, Stafford detention barracks were the anvils on which the national amalgam was forged and shaped". Men pooled stories, discussed plans for the future, got to know each other and each other's possibilities. Furthermore, they fought for better treatment for themselves and they resisted efforts to subdue them. In any case, it was great to receive the military education at England's expense (10).

The internees set up the structure of prisoner governance which was maintained right up to the Northern troubles. The national anthem Amhran na bhFiann (or the Soldier's Song), which was written in 1907, was used as a marching song in the camp and as a result became the de facto national anthem (11). The term 'IRA' which the Volunteers were to become known as during the War of Independence was first introduced in Frongoch as many of the men signed as IRA men in autograph books circulating in the camp (12). A number of leaders of the IRA during the War of Independence 'graduated' from Frongoch, most notably Michael Collins and Dick Mulcahy. These men were largely responsible for directing the military campaign against the British during the War of Independence. Here Collins, who in addition to giving impromptu lessons in guerrilla tactics, even began a list of contacts in preparation for the forthcoming struggle (13). He also made his assessments of the men he later brought together as 'the squad', an elite assassination team most famous for assassinating fifteen of the Cairo Gang (four others were shot and survived) on Bloody Sunday 1920. The Cairo Gang (also referred to as the Murder Gang) was a group of eighteen to twenty plain-clothed British intelligence agents who were sent to Dublin during the Irish War of Independence to carry out intelligence operations against prominent members of the IRA. Another interned here was Arthur Griffith who later headed the delegation to negotiate the treaty with the British government in London. Thirty prisoners later went on to become TDs (14) and one, Sean T O'Kelly, became the second President of Ireland from 1945-1957.

In the aftermath of the Rising, public opinion was not initially on the side of the rebel Volunteers who took part in the insurrection, primarily due to lack of understanding of the purpose, as well as the loss of life, the carnage and bloodshed they created. Captured Volunteers were jeered, abused and pelted with rotten vegetables by 'separation women' (women whose husbands or sons were serving in the British army) when they were being marched through the streets of Dublin. However, this public opinion changed quickly, primarily as a result of the British reaction to the Rising which resulted in sixteen executions which were commuted down from the ninety Volunteers initially sentenced to death. These actions quickly swayed a large section of Irish nationalist opinion away from hostility or ambivalence towards support for the rebels of Easter 1916. In doing so, they galvanised widespread Irish public support and desire for Independence, which ultimately culminated in a landslide victory for Sinn Féin, in the election of 1919. Michael Brennan and his brother, Paddy, amongst others from County Clare, were interned in Frongoch and his account following his release sums up how this change in public opinion presented itself in Limerick.

> I came home around New Year's Day 1917, and I arrived in Limerick on the evening train. We had been "seen off" at Limerick station by a crowd of British soldiers wives ("separation allowance ladies") who howled insults, pelted us with anything handy, and several times had to be forced back physically by the military escort when they tried to get at us with their fists (or nails). Eight months later, when I got off the train in the same station, I was met by a crowd numbering several thousands who cheered themselves hoarse and embarrassed me terribly by carrying me on their shoulders through the streets. It was all very bewildering, but it

> made it clear that the Rising had already changed the people. I spent a few weeks after getting home in making or renewing contacts all over Clare. Everywhere I found enthusiasm and anxiety to be "up and doing", and (now that the prisoners were home) a general expectation that the Volunteers would be re-established on a far bigger scale. (15)

After the Rising and following the release of the Internees from Frongoch the holding of firearms, wearing of uniforms and drilling (training, marching, etc.) of the Volunteers was banned and only carried on in secret. Due to concerns by the Volunteer leadership about how quickly men would tire of the monotony of repetitive secret drill movements and the necessity to stimulate the Volunteers a three-point plan of action was put in place to step up their campaign.

1. Volunteer units to hold drill parades in public preferably in the presence of the RIC.
2. When arrested and charged before a British court the men were to formally refuse to recognise its authority to try them and they were not to plead nor to make any attempt to defend themselves.
3. When sentenced they were to go on hunger strike for political prisoner status (16).

Numerous arrests were made in the area as a result of these activities and the prisoners set about implementing their plan. The British reaction was to release any prisoner who went on hunger strikes when they became sick or got weak and then to re-arrest and re-imprison them after they recovered sufficiently. These actions were carried out under legislation that became known as the 'Cat and Mouse Act'.

As noted earlier, an obituary in a national newspaper states that Johnny was also imprisoned in 1918. I have not been able to validate the accuracy of this article or ascertain where he might have been imprisoned. However, if he was imprisoned at this time it might well have been as a result of the above-mentioned public drilling campaign. As police records at the time show that he, amongst eight or nine others, were named as what the police reports described as 'prominent local Sinn Feiners and Volunteers' who were observed on the 7 December 1916 drilling in the Fianna Hall behind John Daly's house (17). Or alternatively, it could have been as a result of the holding of firearms, as in May 1917 Johnny's workplace was raided and arms were found. However he was not arrested at this time as the following article in the *Limerick Leader* testifies.

> SEIZURE OF ARMS: In Limerick, yesterday morning head constable Price in temporary command of John Street police station with a party of 14 constables, some armed, proceeded to the brush manufacturing establishment of Mr John Mc Sweeney, Mungret Street and searched the premises. Warrant to do so was under the provisions of the Defence of the Realm Act. The police found two revolvers, two air guns, one old pistol and six rounds of revolver ammunition. Those they took with them and also a letter said to be written in Irish. During the search a crowd collected but there was no attempt made at any demonstration. No arrests were made by the Constabulary in connection with the search (18).

Chapter 6

Activities During The War Of Independence

The Irish War of Independence began in January 1919 in Solohead in Co. Tipperary where two RIC officers were shot. The episode led to the gradual development of an intense campaign with the IRA adopting guerrilla war tactics against the superior military might of the British establishment.

Witness statements or other documents that I have read do not detail any specific military operations in which Johnny was involved. But to a large degree, it is not surprising that no mention exists because, as explained in the next two chapters, for a large element of the War of Independence Johnny was interned without trial in various prisons and an internment camp. Having read many of these statements, and in light of the facts below, I believe it would be safe to deduce that if Johnny did not specifically partake in some or any of the actions attributable to his battalion or the wider brigade area, he would have been very much involved in the planning and implementation of these operations, given:

- His central role in the setting up of the Volunteers in the city.

- His eagerness to partake in the Rising in which he was one of the six who voted for an insurrection in the city in 1916. Even though he had full knowledge of the overwhelming military strength of the Crown forces in the city and the lack of arms due to the sinking of the *Aud*.
- His role as a senior officer, firstly as a captain of B Company and then Vice-Commandant of the 2nd Battalion, effectively making him second in charge of the City Volunteers which numbered over 400 men [1].
- His documented central role in the setting up of the 2nd Battalion in the city which in large measure was attributed to him following the split in the City Battalion caused as a result of their perceived inaction in the Easter Rising [2].
- His senior role in the membership of the IRB in the region which culminated in him at an early date, prior to the Easter Rising becoming head centre for an IRB circle in the city. Their IRB's stated role was the overthrow of the English government by force of arms and of establishing an Irish Republic.
- His arrest and long-term internment in two different prisons/camps and at least three others (Cork Prison, Kilworth detention Camp and Limerick Prison) for shorter periods of time.
- The references to him 'not seeking the limelight, working fearlessly in the background arming (purchasing) and training men' and 'There was only one goal for him –freedom. He would have preferred to breathe pure free Irish air and be in want than to occupy the highest position in the land and have Ireland in subjection' [3].
- He would have been well associated with many individuals attached to the 2nd Battalion (and indeed in the wider Mid-West region) who gave detailed accounts of military operations. He was in a number of cases a captain of the battalion involved in the operations.
- It is documented in his obituary which was written by a colleague of his, Michael Hartney who was captain of E-Company and who was arrested and sent to Wormwood Scrubs along with Johnny that.

'When activity was on the quiet side Johnny set to work to build up a strong body of men who would fearlessly espouse the cause of 'Roisin Dhu'* (*a metaphor for Ireland) in the struggle that he seemed to visualise years before it actually came. He never sought the limelight was content to fill the role of promoter until his undoubted abilities could no longer be overlooked and he was compelled to accept the Vice-Commandant position of the Battalion (2nd). Night and day he was on the alert to further the project of arming others who were under his command while he was ever insistent that discipline should be instilled into the Volunteers through the medium of ceremonial drill' (4).

- Liam Ford one of his commanding officers stated that Johnny was one of the most active members of the Brigade (5).
- His activities were observed by and were well known to the British authorities. An army/police intelligence document dated 13 April 1920 stated that in addition to being aware that Johnny was an officer in the 2nd Battalion it also stated that he 'was capable of carrying out outrages' (6). Furthermore, as noted in the last chapter, in December 1916 a police report also observed and noted Johnny as partaking in drilling in the back of John Daly's house in Barrington Street and in May 1917 his house was raided by fourteen RIC officers who found arms.

As noted above Johnny was promoted to Vice-Commandant of the 2nd Battalion. He obtained this position after his release from Ballykinlar (see paragraph 8). He was, prior to this, Company Captain of B-Company (7).

The above-mentioned Michael Hartney in his witness statement gives an interesting account of an altercation he had with RIC officers on 13 October 1920, in which he mentions Johnny.

'While waiting for one of my men who had borrowed my gun, I was chatting with the Vice-Commandant of the 2nd Battalion (Sean Mac Sweeney) when from apparently nowhere four R.I.C. men confronted me and demanded I put up my hands. I refused and they caught my arms and proceeded to take me to jail. This happened in Carr St. Limerick. On the way to the William St. Police Barracks, I threw the two R.I.C. men who held my arms and ran. They opened fire, sending 8 rounds after me, one of which I received in the right heel. Feeling myself getting weak, I ran into a house, out to the yard in the hope of climbing to safety by the wall, but fell and was again in custody. This happened on the 13th October 1920, and I was interned in Bere Island, after having been carried around as a hostage for six months. The order, every time I was put on a lorry, was "In case of attack shoot the hostage" (8).

I recall my father informing me of such hostage-taking occurring and that at times these hostages were tied to the front of vehicles.

RIC military vehicles and armoured car leaving Limerick on a scouting expedition with a prisoner hostage in the front vehicle.
(Courtesy of the National Library of Ireland-colourising commissioned by author)

The activities in the War of Independence started in the Limerick city area on 6 April 1919 (9). This incident related to the arrest of the battalion adjutant Robert Byrne, for having a revolver which was found in his house during a police raid. Byrne was sentenced to twelve months in jail in Limerick Prison. A month later he and fellow Republican prisoners went on hunger strike because they were denied political status. However, his health deteriorated quickly and he was removed under guard from prison to the City Home Hospital, then known at the Limerick Union Workhouse. The 2nd Battalion command, seeing this as an opportunity, decided to organise a rescue attempt but it failed as Byrne was shot and died and a RIC officer was also killed in the incident. This episode resulted in the British forces proclaiming Limerick a Special Military Area which placed the city under martial law. The social ramification of this action resulted in the famous Limerick Soviet which was effectively a two-week general strike in the city against British rule.

It would appear that Johnny and his brother Paddy knew Byrne well as Paddy's son, Terry, recalled to me that a picture of Byrne hung in their family home. Indeed, an account suggests that Johnny had a central role in the authorisation of this operation. Michael Stack, a member of E-Company who took part in this rescue operation and who shot the RIC officer, states in his witness statement that the rescue attempt was sanctioned by the 2nd Battalion staff. He also confirms that Johnny was a member of this staff at the time of the rescue (10). Furthermore, the rescue was carried out by B and C Company and Johnny was captain of B Company at this time. From this date on through until the start of the following year (1920) the activities of the 2nd Battalion were quiet (11).

The following is a list in chronological order of the activities that took place in the Limerick city area while Johnny was not interned which I have obtained from Thomas Toomey's book *War of*

Independence in Limerick (12). But as stated above, I have found no documented evidence of him partaking in any of these activities.

31 January 1920   A concerted attack on Murroe RIC Barracks by the Mid-Limerick Brigade. The attack failed but was a signal of things to come. Interestingly, this was the day Johnny was arrested and sent to Wormwood Scrubs (see next paragraph).

19 May 1920   Two Officers shot dead in an ambush in Mallow Street. This was shortly after Johnny's release from Wormwood Scrubs.

1 June 1920.   The idea of forming a flying column is conceived.

12 June 1920   An RIC man shot dead in the Railway Hotel, Parnell Street by Volunteer Patrick Naughton. Naughton is buried in the Republican Plot having been killed in the Civil War in the battle for Limerick City (13).

22 June 1920   A daring attack on three Black and Tans was carried out in broad daylight in Henry Street in which one was shot dead and the other two disarmed. The attackers faced with the problem of retreating troops and crowded streets decided to separate and one of them dropped his revolver into a pillar box on the street corner. Next morning when the postman opened the box, he was confronted by members of the IRA (14).

Activities during the War of Independence

11 September 1920 Newly formed Mid-Limerick Flying Column attempts its first ambush at Ballinagarde, near Ballyneety.

8 November 1920 East Limerick and Mid-Limerick flying columns combine to mount a major ambush at Grange near Bruff. However, instead of the expected two lorries of Black and Tans, the lorries contained RAF men in transit. With great difficulty, they managed to extricate themselves having seriously wounded a British officer.

27 November 1920 A daring assassination attempt virtually at the gates of the barracks in Limerick is carried out by an IRA unit but the intended target, who was one of the most notorious members of the British headquarters staff and was in charge of British intelligence, escapes.

CHAPTER 7

INTERNMENT IN WORMWOOD SCRUBS

Some months after the outbreak of the War of Independence, Johnny was arrested, along with twelve of his Mid-Limerick Brigade comrades, in what the *Limerick Leader* described as 'an extensive raid in Limerick in the early hours of Saturday the 31st of January 1920'. They were arrested under what was known as the 'Defence of the Realm Act' which effectively permitted the authorities to arrest, detain and incarcerate without trial any persons suspected of being involved in activities that would endanger the Union. No specific reason or incident is recorded for their arrest. However, a military records report cited the following 'that they are persons who are suspected of acting and having acted and of being about to act in a manner prejudicial to the public safety and Defence of the Realm'.

They were conveyed under an escort of police and military with two tanks to the railway station and left Limerick on the 8.50 a.m. train to Cork where they were detained in prison [1]. They remained there until the following Sunday week, 8 February, after which, according to the *Limerick Leader*, they were deported to Wormwood

Scrubs Prison in London at 5 o'clock in the morning. Their removal was described as a carefully planned military operation with a big force of military and a number of policemen present. They were taken to Cobh, or Queenstown as it was known then, where they were transferred in secrecy onto one of the two naval ships which lay awaiting the men. The secrecy was, assumedly to minimise the risk of attack. Both ships then left at the same time, their destination in England at that time not known (2).

Conditions in Wormwood Scrubs Prison would at that time have been quite harsh as in addition to being interned without trial far from home, they had to experience at close quarters regular hardened criminals with serious convictions. The prison was described as being:

> ....a cold, wet place, the walls excluded water all the time (3)......... on entering the large entrance hall it was like a scene from another world. The putrid smell of foul air, a mixture of oakum and decay, of sweating and sick humanity, was choking. A dark yellow fog made everything dim and it took some moments to distinguish the surroundings. For some minutes, we were standing there and, in that time, a file of about ten miserable prisoners passed slowly along in front of us. They were small in size, deformed some of them very lame, others of them hunchbacked and each of them was carrying an iron ball which was chained to his leg. Their movements were deadly slow, their faces were drained of blood, flesh-parched and furrowed (4).

Amongst those arrested along with Johnny that morning were Peter (or Peader) Dunne, a veteran of the 1916 Rising in Dublin who was at that time the officer commanding the Mid-Limerick Brigade (5), James Gubbins Adjutant of the same Brigade, Patrick Whelan (an uncle of Bill Whelan of Riverdance notoriety – see the copy of his internment order on page 63) and Michael Hartney who was captain of E-Company of the 2nd Battalion. The latter three later provided witness statements but only Michael Hartney gives some detail of the events that occurred whilst in Wormwood Scrubs but he along with Gubbins was transferred shortly after arrival to Brixton Prison. However, he does state that a hunger strike was started on 18 March 1920. The hunger strike related to an attempt to obtain information as to the whereabouts of the prison commandant of Wormwood Scrubs, who was taken from jail in the early hours of the morning. After four days on hunger strike, they appeared to have some success as his location was finally disclosed as Brixton Prison. Tom Byrne, Peter Dunne, Seamus Dunne and Michael Hartney were transferred to keep him company (6). Johnny remained in Wormwood Scrubs where he took part in the ongoing hunger strikes in the prison.

In his research paper titled 'The eyes of the Irish world are watching -Sinn Féin Hunger strikes in Britain', Gerard Noonan of Trinity College Dublin documented (7);

> In the subsequent four months (i.e. after February), Wormwood Scrubs experienced four hunger strikes pursued in order to secure such aims as better treatment, prisoner of war status and unconditional release. The shortest strike lasted a day-and-a-half; the longest twenty-two days. The number of prisoners involved varied between one and one hundred and ninety-two. The fourth strike ended when the internees were moved to convalescing homes around London. Although they were still detained, many of the prisoners pre-empted the British government by simply walking out of hospital when they had sufficiently recovered from their ordeal. Taken in by the London Irish, they eventually made their way home.

According to accounts, the authorities tried several stunts to try to break the hunger strikes. They put steaming kippers into the cells, to which the prisoners responded by breaking the window and throwing the suppers out. They also brought what was described as a 'special man from the Home Office' to address them

Internment in Wormwood Scrubs

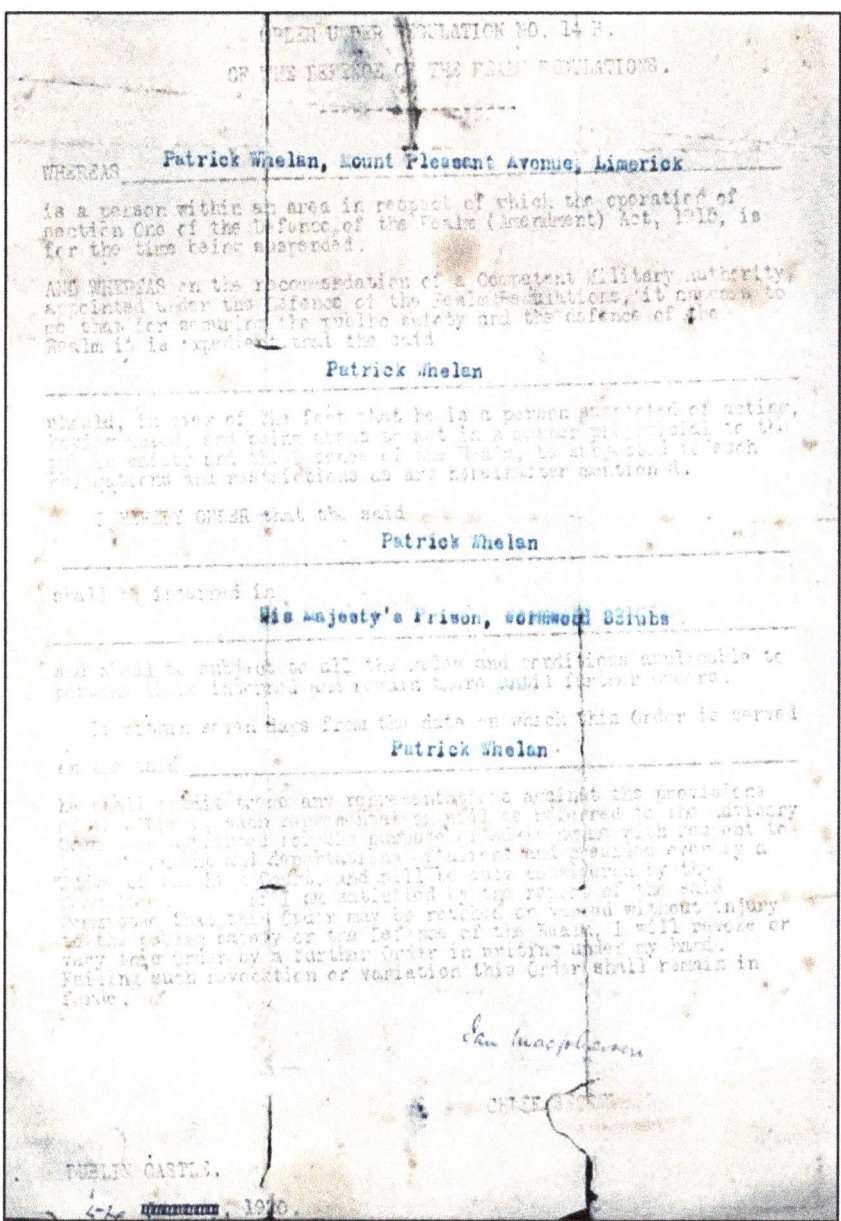

Copy of the original internment order that was served on Patrick Whelan, who was arrested on the same morning as Johnny, which is on display in the Limerick City Museum. My transcript of the wording is shown on the next page. This order effectively meant imprisonment without trial for an unspecified period of time. *(Courtesy Limerick Museum)*

The Forgotten Vice-Commandant

ORDER UNDER REGULATION NO. 14 B.
OF THE DEFENCE OF THE REALM REGULATIONS

Whereas **Patrick Whelan, Mount Pleasant Avenue, Limerick**
Is a person within an area in respect of which the operation of section 1 of the defence of the realm (amendment) Act, 1915, is for the time being suspended.
AND WHEREAS on the recommendation of a competent Military Authority appointed under the defence of the Realm Regulations it appears to me that for securing the public safety and the Defence of the Realm it is expedient that the said

Patrick Whelan

Should in view of the fact that he is a person suspected of acting, have acted, and been about the act in a manner prejudicial to the public safety and the defence of the relevant regulations, be subject to such obligations and restrictions as hereunder mentioned.

I HEREBY ORDER that the Said
Patrick Whelan

Shall be interned in
His Majesty's Prison Wormwood Scrubs
And shall be subject to all the rules and conditions applicable to persons there interned and remain there until further orders.

If within served days of the date on which this order is served
on the said _____ **Patrick Whelan**

He shall submit to me any representations against the provisions of this order, such representations will be referred to the advisory committee appointed for the purpose of advising me with respect to this internment and deportation of aliens and presided over by a Judge of the high court, and will be duly considered by the Committee, if I am satisfied by the report of the said Committee that this order may be revoked without injury to the public safety or the Defence of the Realm, I will revoke or vary this order by a further order in writing under my hand failing such revocation or variation this order still remains in force.

CHIEF SECRETARY
DUBLIN CASTLE
???????1920

Transcript of the internment order on the previous page

and promise all sorts of concessions if they went off the strike. They tried to induce the prisoners to come out of their cells to the exercise compound to hear him, but their answer was to remain in bed (8). An article in the *Limerick Leader* describes the conditions that the internees endured;

> Most of the men, who now number 96 are confined to the cells and are not allowed visits from their friends. The wardens continue to tempt the dying men with appetising food, but is all of no avail. The condition of the majority of the men is pitiable, and their barbarous and inhumane treatment at the hands of the British government is a disgrace to civilisation. This is the 20th day of the hunger strike. A visitor to the prison said that the condition of these men was absolutely appalling. They were reeling around the prison yard, he stated, like hopelessly drunken men clutching at the iron railings to keep themselves from falling. They stagger for a few yards, then rest against the walls then grip the railings for a minute or two. While they are talking to each other their bodies are swaying, whilst their legs are crumbling under them. Still, there is no intention of surrender. The cry is "death before surrender" and we will fight on. The men feel, writes the London correspondent of the "Freeman" that the government will continue their torture until they have killed them or permanently ruined their health (9).

In Johnny's case, the final sentence of the above article came to pass. According to her pension application, Johnny's wife, Kate states that he spent seventeen to twenty days on hunger strike. She noted that this resulted in the origin of his stomach trouble from which he was never to recover as he was constantly in ill health from this time until he died some sixteen months later (10).

Numerous articles appeared in the national and international press highlighting the plight of the hunger strikers which brought international attention. On one occasion, 20,000 Irishmen and women from all parts of London made an impressive demonstration outside the prison.

Limerick Corporation councillors' passed a motion to bring their plight to the attention of all foreign ambassadors in London.

> Asking them to do all in their power to secure that these men be treated with humanity and justice and thus add strength to the protest that has already been made by 88 elected representatives of the American people in their recent cable (telegram) to the British Premier (11).

Johnny was released on temporary parole on 27 March 1920 to look after his sick wife (12). At this time, Kate was expecting her youngest son Robert (Bertie) who was born just days later on 3 April 1920. Johnny was subsequently granted two extensions of his parole and although he would have been entitled to a further extension, he returned on 29 April of his own free will to re-join his suffering comrades on their hunger strike (13). Johnny's return on this date coincided with a major well-publicised demonstration by over 5,000 supporters outside the prison which ended in skirmishes with the police. A newspaper article reported that the secretary of the self-determination league (a body set up in Britain to work for the independence of the Irish nation) who was addressing the demonstration announced through a megaphone to the assembled crowd that Johnny and another comrade from Co. Cork who were released on parole were present. He also revealed that they were returning to prison and it was their intention to go on hunger strike immediately when they went in (14). At this demonstration, pamphlets were handed out which stated the following.

> ARE THEY TO DIE?- In Wormwood Scrubs Jail over 100 Irish men are dying. In prison for months without charge or trial. They are now protesting in the only effective way left to honourable men. There are on hunger strike as a protest against the imprisonment without charge or trial, and they will die sooner than submit any longer to a terrible tyranny which is worst that Russia under the

Internment in Wormwood Scrubs

CHEERING THE SINN FEIN PRISONERS AT WORMWOOD SCRUBS. Sympathisers with the Sinn Fein prisoners who have been on hunger strike at Wormwood Scrubs gathered outside the famous London prison with flags and musical instruments to cheer and encourage their incarcerated compatriots. (1) Girls with flags arriving at the prison. (2) A responding wave of the Irish flag from a window of the prison.

Newspaper cutting from April 1920 about the protests from the *Times Weekly Edition Illustrated Section*.

(Author's original paper cutting)

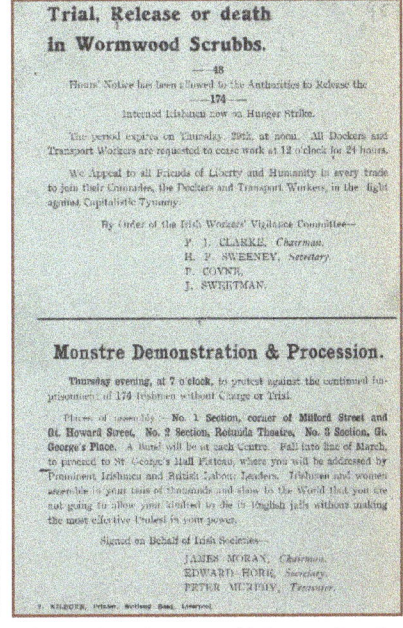

Image of a demonstration outside the prison showing a self-determination league protestor speaking to the prisoners through a megaphone and an advertisement for the demonstration planned for the date that Johnny returned to Wormwood Scrubs.

(Courtesy of the National Library of Ireland HOG_147)

> Czar. If these men die? Come in your thousands to Wormwood Scrubs every night at 7:30 PM, to demand the release of these men (15).

Following his return, the authorities began to release the prisoners in batches and take them to various hospitals around London. Johnny was discharged from Wormwood Scrubs to Cornwallis Infirmary – essentially a workhouse- for convalescing on 10 May 1920 where he was photographed with other inmates. My grandmother had this picture on prominent display in our family home. A medical officer's report stated that Johnny, along with twenty-six others was conveyed from the prison on that date in ambulances along with a hospital warden and the medical officer. The report further stated that all patients showed considerable signs of weakness but refused all nourishment until arrival at the hospital (16).

The following account about Johnny's time in prison was written in later years by his battalion friend and comrade Michael Hartney who was interned along with Johnny;

> When the enemy closed her prison doors on those of the IRA who fell into her hands, and when things were anything but pleasant for those who occupied the cells prepared for them by the English. It was not unnatural that a feeling of gloom and hopelessness was often encountered when speaking to some of the men who later wrote big names in Irish history. It was here that "Johnny" was perhaps at his best. No despondency for him. On the contrary, he was planning for things that could be done on release, suggesting schemes for recruiting or organising; always encouraging others and pointing out that determination was more than half success. In short he was an optimist where freedom was concerned, and his knowledge of Wolfe Tone was his guiding light in everything national. No better or truer pal could one have in jail. A half cigarette would be divided; everything that was considered a luxury would be shared; he was the personification of unselfishness and generosity (17).

Internment in Wormwood Scrubs

Photograph taken in May 1920 in Cornwallis Infirmary, Islington, London. Johnny is pictured on the back row third from left. See link in end notes for names of all internees in photograph (18) *(Family photograph)*

As noted, these hunger strikes helped bring some international attention to the Irish struggle, but later on that year, the most famous hunger strike of the period was begun by the Mayor of Cork Terence MacSwiney. He was arrested by the British on charges of sedition or incitement or resistance to lawful authority, on 16 August 1920 and sentenced to two years imprisonment in Brixton Prison in England. He immediately began a hunger strike in protest at his internment and his trial by a military court. He died there in October 1920 after seventy-four days on hunger strike and his death catapulted him and the Irish struggle for independence to prominent international attention [19]. Indeed, the then King, George V, was considering over-ruling Prime Minister Lloyd George's refusal to release MacSwiney, thereby threatening a constitutional crisis. MacSwiney also greatly influenced well-known international figures such as Indian revolutionaries, Mahatma Gandhi, who led India to independence and, Jawaharlal Nehru, India's First Prime Minister. Ho Chi Minh, the Vietnamese Communist revolutionary leader who later became a Prime Minister of his country, was an admirer who was working in London at the time of MacSwiney's death and he famously declared that 'a nation that has such citizens will never surrender [20].

I have firm recollections of Terence MacSwiney's name being frequently spoken with reverence by my grandmother and my father in our family home. I suspect that Johnny may have known him well. As I mentioned in Chapter four he would have met him in John Daly's house. In addition, he was also a member of the IRB and, as mentioned earlier, the IRB Divisional Centre for Munster held their meetings in Limerick. Johnny likely felt a deep degree of empathy with him following his own participation in the hunger strikes in Wormwood Scrubs earlier that year. This empathy is reflected in a *Limerick Leader* article, which appeared a month before

MacSwiney's death. It stated that a Board of Guardians meeting, which Johnny presided over as vice-chairman, was adjourned following a unanimous motion, in protest at the treatment of Alderman T. MacSwiney, Lord Mayor of Cork and other prisoners on hunger strike [21].

CHAPTER 8

INTERNMENT IN BALLYKINLAR

In a reprisal for the assassination carried out by the IRA of fourteen undercover British intelligence agents, known as the Cairo or Murder Gang, in Dublin in the early morning of Sunday the 21 November 1920, British soldiers indiscriminately fired at spectators attending a football match between Dublin and Tipperary in Croke Park killing fourteen innocent civilians. Later on that day in Dublin Castle, they also tortured and murdered three IRA men arrested the night before following the Cairo Gang assassinations. In the aftermath of these events, later known as 'Bloody Sunday', a decision was made to initiate large-scale arrests for what was described as '2,000 of the most active gunmen'. Widespread arrests of known republican activists throughout the country occurred under a new law known as the Restoration of Order in Ireland Regulations and internment camps were opened throughout the country [1]. Johnny and his brothers Paddy and Denis were arrested sometime before the end of November [2] and sent to Ballykinlar Internment Camp in County Down which opened the following month [3]. They arrived at Ballykinlar on 11 December [4]. This internment effectively ended Johnny's active role in the War of Independence as he was not released until after the signing of the Treaty in December 1921.

Located on a bleak, sandy and marshy landscape in the shadow of the Mourne Mountains in County Down, Ballykinlar had a reputation for brutality (5). Three prisoners were shot dead for minor infractions, such as standing too close to the barbed wire fence that kept them penned in, while five died from malnutrition (6). Johnny, having been arrested at the end of November, would have been one of the early prisoners to arrive and was placed in hut number eighteen of Camp One (7). Camp Two was opened at a later date – the camps were referred to as cages by the inmates. It was the first centre of mass internment in Ireland and housed over 2,000 men over a twelve-month period (8).

Johnny and his two brothers followed the typical path to Ballykinlar that internees arrested from the north Munster area travelled. From Limerick Prison or RIC Barracks they were detained for a period in Kilworth Camp, County Cork for questioning and then transferred to Cork Prison (9). To minimise the risk of ambush, they were transferred by ship to Belfast on military vessels which were at sea for two-and-a-half days. The following is a witness statement account of the journey from Limerick to Cork.

> In a convoy of fourteen lorries armoured cars etc. We set out from the New Barracks, Limerick (now known as Sarsfield Barracks). And again heard the order issued to the escort to shoot the prisoners in case of ambush. In the absence of perfection of the internal combustion engine at the time, it was understandable that cars were breaking down every few miles of the road. It took a day to reach Buttevant from Limerick, where we halted for the night and had an early start the following morning. At the start the officer instructed the escort, if attacked to use the prisoners as cover or as shield. There was the usual number of halts for repairs on the way and I recall that between Mallow and Cork we were halted on the road for a considerable time, while the

snow came down. It was a miracle that nobody collapsed under such trying circumstances. It was after dark when we reached Cork, and Patrick St. was still smouldering from the intense bombardment of a few days before. We were brought to Cork Jail at Sunday's Well (10).

An account of the conditions the internees then endured on the ship from Cork to Belfast recalls;

> We were housed right at the bottom of the craft and were right up against the iron walls of the ship, the floor being only five or six feet wide immediately over the keel. The air was foul and cold and for the next two-and-a-half days, we had to endure this. We were brought on deck once for a breather. Many of the lads got very sick, which was not surprising under the circumstances. We got very little food all this time, a few very hard biscuits and a bucket of hot tea, insufficient to make the rounds (11).

Accounts also state that, upon arrival in Belfast, they were then greeted by angry and hostile unionist shipyard workers who with chants of 'What will de Valera do for ye now', threw steel bars at the internees who were tightly packed into lorries, causing injury. They were then brought away in these lorries to the Belfast and County Down Railway Station (Belfast's Queen's Quay Station which is now closed) where they then travelled by train to Ballykinlar Halt Railway Station (12).

Upon arrival at this station, early prisoners, some of whom were suffering from untreated injuries sustained from the shipyard workers attacks had to then march, handcuffed in pairs carrying their luggage, for three miles to the camp. They were then placed in bare huts with nothing to sleep in except damp straw and had to endure additional hardships such as inadequate food (13). In addition, they were not allowed to receive parcels of food from family and had to fight for proper camp conditions from which the later prisoners benefited.

Internment in Ballykinlar

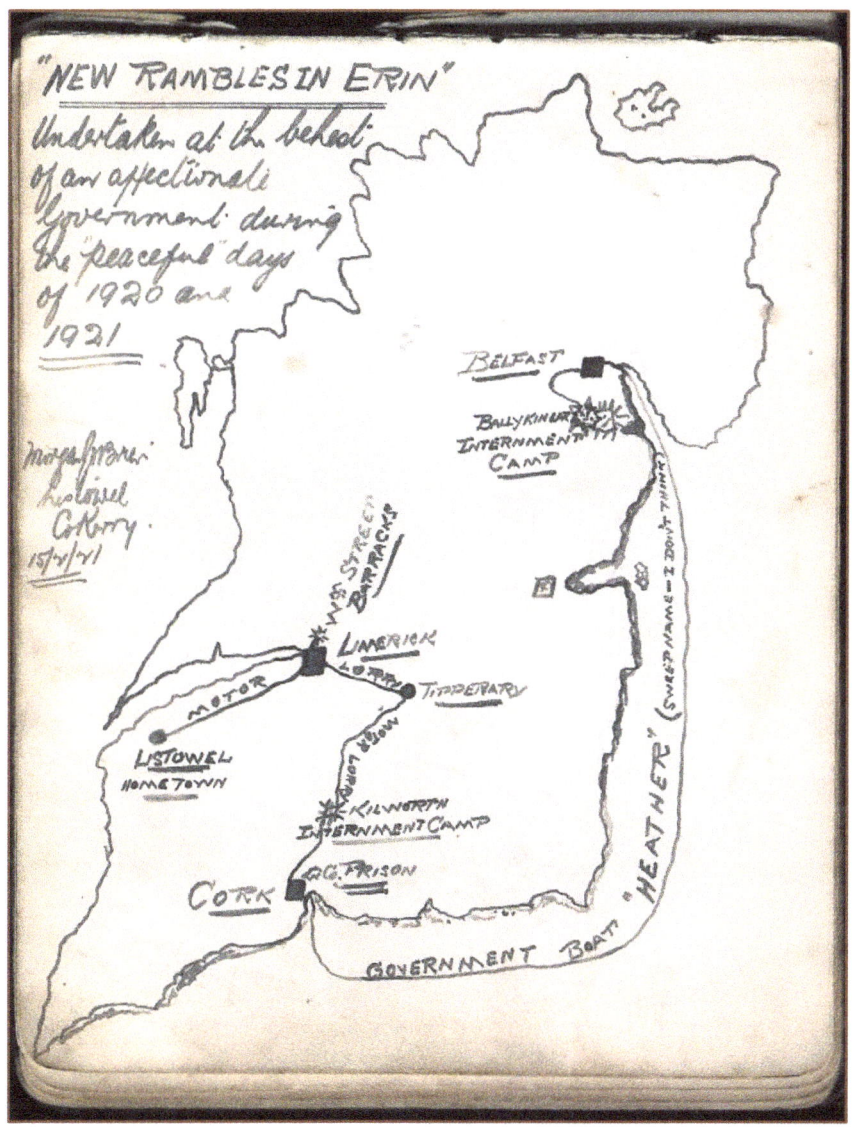

Drawing from an autograph book showing the route of the trip to Ballykinlar made by a Kerry internee.

(Source of image unknown)

A former IRA prisoner, Derry man Louis J. Walsh who later became a judge was interned in Hut Nineteen next to Johnny's Hut. He published a book in 1921 about his experiences in various institutions in the North of Ireland including a chapter about his time in Ballykinlar Camp. He describes the conditions he found upon his arrival sometime after the early hard-won concessions were obtained.

> The huts were zinc buildings, our beds were composed of two wooden trestles about eight inches high with three boards laid on top, on which we placed our bedding, consisting of a mattress and bolster packed with coarse straw and four army blankets; and the other furniture comprised a long table, three or four forms, some shelving, a few buckets, etc., and a stove (14).
>
> The internees ran both Camps along military lines. They had their own government, police forces, military, courts post office and currency. The most important executive officers of our government were the Line Captains. (A line comprised ten huts in each of which there were supposed to be twenty-five men). Each line constituted a Company and had a captain in charge of it. The knowledge and skills possessed by the diverse inhabitants were used to teach classes, and other activities, such as sports, drama and music lessons, helped stave off boredom (15).

Johnny's Company was known as C-Company and there were four lines of huts (or companies) in each camp (see image on page 89). The Camp One commandant was Joe Mc Grath from Dublin who was also a TD. Johnny would have been well acquainted with this man as both of them were also interned together in Wormwood Scrubs (16).

The internees also endeavoured to defy their captors with various escape plans. Some of these involved tunnelling under the wire, however, Ballykinlar Camp was constructed close to a beach and thus had sandy soil. Following a number of attempts, it was discovered that these soil conditions made tunnelling impossible (17). However, one attempt in Camp One came close to success and an account states;

> The will to be free was ever dominant in the minds of the internees and, with this end always in view, many attempts were made to get

Internment in Ballykinlar

Image of Camp 1

(Courtesy of Down County Museum)

Images of Camp 1

(Courtesy of Kilmainham Jail Gaol Museum/ OPW 19P0-1A32-07)

out of the camp. One effort worth recording was made from Hut 2. A trap-door was very cleverly cut out in the wash-up room of this hut and the making of a tunnel was commenced. Hut 2 was in an extreme position in the camp just inside the barbed wire barricades, and almost under the sentry box. The tunnelling was carried on almost day and night and the sand - it was on ground of a sandy nature - was taken out and disposed of in various places all over the camp. To prevent the sandy sides and top of the tunnel from subsiding it had to be lined with boards, mostly bed-boards. The passage had been made for more than a hundred yards to a point under a fence which would afford shelter from view, when the Truce was announced on 11th July 1921. Fearing that any attempt to escape at this juncture would involve breaking the conditions of the Truce, a communication was sent to G.H.Q. for instructions. Before any reply had been received, an escape took place from the Curragh, and as a precaution against such a thing happening at Ballykinlar, the camp authorities immediately dug a trench over four feet deep around the camp, which rendered the discovery of the tunnel inevitable. There was just time to recall some men who were at work in the tunnel. The candles they were using, however, were lighting when the soldiers broke in, some shouting that the place was equipped with electric light. Wooden rails were laid on the bottom of the tunnel and a wooden bogey was pulled in and out with a long cord or rope. In this way, the sand excavated was brought in and then disposed of all over the camp. Needless to say, the discovery of the tunnel was a great disappointment, but other attempts were made, and another tunnel was discovered when a heavy military lorry went down through the roadway at the point where the tunnel undermined it (18).

OPPOSITE
Photograph of Johnny (third from left second last row) and his fellow Hut 18 internees pictured in Ballykinlar. His brother Denis is also pictured (third from left on the first row). There is also an Edward Mc Sweeney listed on the second row third from the left which I initially felt was a typo and may have been Paddy but I have been unable to have this verified as there was also an unrelated Eamon Mc Sweeney in the hut.
(Photograph courtesy of Conor Boyle whose grandfather Captain James Boyle from Donegal is also pictured on the left second row from front)

The Forgotten Vice-Commandant

The photo on the previous page has a mounting border which I omitted for clarity titled;

BALLYKINLAR INTERNMENT CAMP
NO.1
IRISH REPUBLICAN PRISONERS, 1920-1921
HUT 18-"C" COMPANY

It also lists each internee which I have included in footnote [19].

This image was taken by a professional photographer Frank Mc Kay, Dolphins Barn, Dublin, who was himself interned at Ballykinlar in Hut Fourteen. Frank who photographed all the internees in each hut, arranged for a friend on the outside to bake a small fold-up camera into a cake and post it into the camp.

Louis J. Walsh's book also describes in some detail the brutal shooting of two men, Joseph Tormey and Patrick Sloane from Westmeath in Camp One which would have occurred on 17 January, some six or seven weeks after Johnny's arrival in the camp.

> …..a few days after our coming No. 2 Camp was opened and began to fill up rapidly. Portion of this camp adjoined ours and was only separated from us by a barbed-wire fence. Along this fence on our side was a macadamised road, which we used as a promenade. As was naturally to be expected, we were in the habit of talking through the fence to our acquaintances on the other side, and at first no objection was made to this practice. Sometimes, however, groups would gather on each side, and in their eagerness to get talking with each other prisoners would occasionally get very close to the wires. We were forbidden to approach within arm's reach of the fence; and when they considered that we were too near, the sentries would order us back. In the beginning the thing was done in a good-natured sort of way; but then we noticed that the sentries were getting rather aggressive. We believed that they were acting under the inspiration of some of their junior officers as somebody overheard one of these say to a sentry, who complained to him that the prisoners were coming too close: "You

Internment in Ballykinlar

Artwork from the Book of Ballykinlar showing camp life
(Courtesy Military Archives ref. IE-MA-PRCN-0020-01-03)

Artwork from the Book of Ballykinlar showing the inside of a typical hut
(Courtesy Military Archives ref. IE-MA-PRCN-0020-01-03)

have your rifle and you know what it is for! " Finally, two or three shots were fired by sentries on different occasions; and one of these, at least, was fired at a time when there was nobody nearer the wires than the middle of the road. Our Commandant, Patrick Colgan, complained to the British Commandant of the action of the sentries; but the latter pooh-poohed the idea that the shots were fired to hit. Mr. Colgan said that, if it was not permitted to the prisoners to speak into the other camp, or even to use the road, Colonel Little had only to say so, and an order would forthwith be issued by the prisoners' Commandant to that effect. But the Colonel said that he did not wish any such thing, that he did not expect impossibilities, and that the prisoners were quite at liberty to use the road for any purpose so long as they did not approach any nearer than within three feet of the wires. Just about mid-day on that day (Monday), I was in my hut when I heard a shot ring out. I paid no attention to it at first, for shots from sentries were beginning to get common, as I have explained. Then, I saw somebody running, and the news came along the line that two men were killed. When I got up beside Hut II I found that practically the whole camp had gathered and that the men were on their knees saying the Rosary. It was a moment of terrible excitement and deep emotion, and the sight of our two comrades lying in their blood was something calculated to sweep off their feet the calmest of men. I never heard that during the great European war was the allegation made in respect of Germans, Turks, Bulgars, Frenchmen, Englishmen, or anybody else that they had shot, out of hand, unarmed and defenceless prisoners behind barbed wire; and everybody was so stirred by the brutality of the affair that anything might have happened that day"..........
"Medical evidence showed that the bullet hit one of the prisoners on the right side of the head, and passing to the other prisoner in the neck killing both. The British claimed that the men were too close to the fence. Witnesses, as was evident, from the pools of blood on the roadway testified that these two prisoners were nowhere near the fence at the time of the shooting [20].

In an interesting twist of faith some two weeks later, 150 miles south of Ballykinlar, in Dromkeen, County Limerick a similar fate was to befall two Black and Tans at the hands of a combined operation by

Internment in Ballykinlar

Photograph and artwork of the memorial outside Hut No. 11 where Tormay and Sloane were shot.
(Courtesy of Kilmainham Gaol Museum/ OPW 19P0-1A32-0)

The Forgotten Vice-Commandant

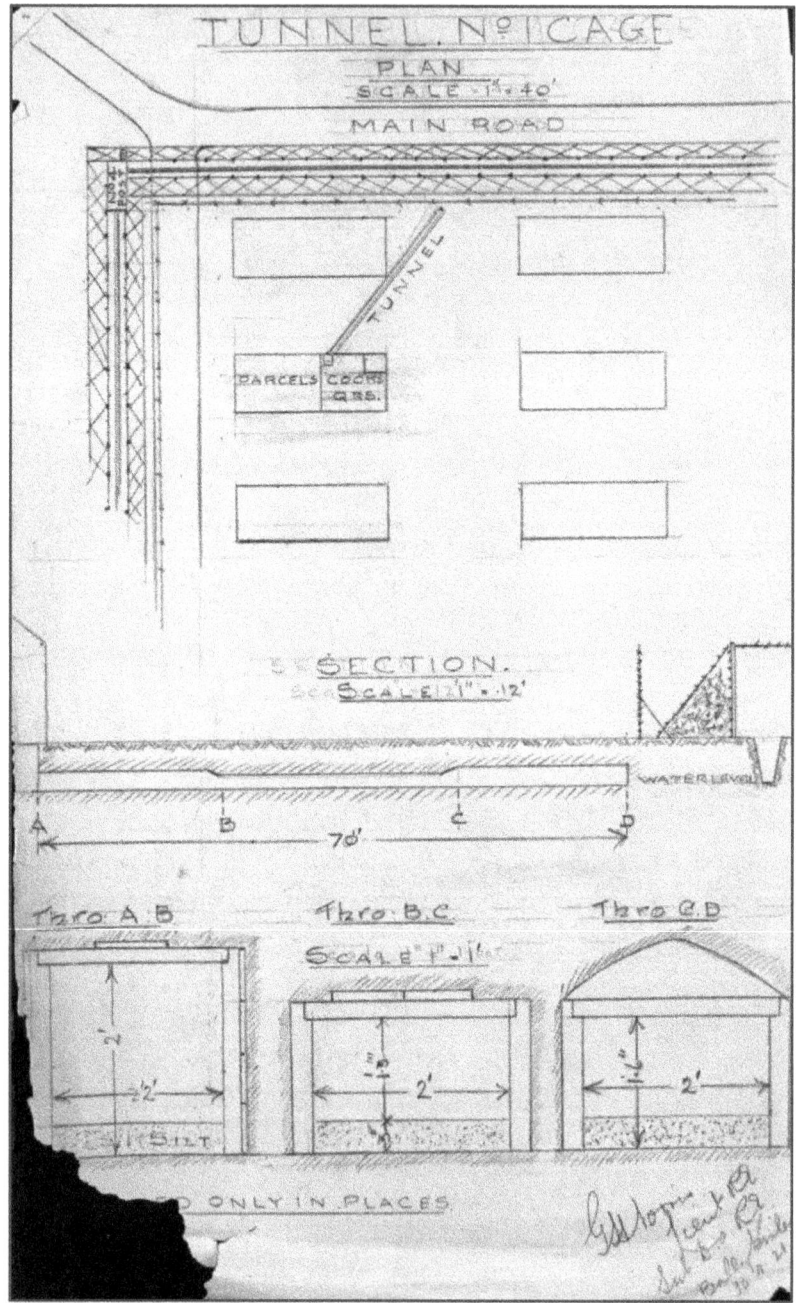

Copy of an extract from a camp report investigating the second tunnel mentioned in the previous statement which details that tunnel's construction (*Image reproduced by courtesy of The National Archives, London, England W035/145/00844*)

Johnny's comrades in the Mid-Limerick Brigade and the East Limerick Brigade. In what was the largest loss of life in an ambush outside of County Cork in the War of Independence (21). A Volunteer, under instruction, to execute the two surviving soldiers of nine RIC and Black and Tans, who were killed in the ambush, lined up the two soldiers together and shot them both dead with one bullet through their heads (22).

Later on that year on 15 November, another internee, Tadhg Barry from Cork who was returning to his quarters after saying goodbye to a group of internees being released was shot dead by a nervous young sentry. Barry was highly respected in Cork and was an Alderman and secretary of the ITGWU union in Cork. The respect in which he was held is evident by the fact that amongst those who attended his funeral was Michael Collins, who broke from the Treaty talks in London to return home for the occasion.

As noted earlier, Johnny's continuing ill health since his hunger strike in Wormwood Scrubs would also plague him during this period of internment. His wife, Kate, stated in her pension application that he was attended to by fellow internee Dr Richard Hayes (23). At that time Hayes was a Sinn Féin TD for Limerick East. He participated in the 1916 Rising in Ashbourne where he received a capital sentence which was commuted to twenty years penal servitude (24). He later became the Irish Film Censor from 1941 to 1954, as well as Director of the Abbey Theatre.

During this time of internment, Johnny carved a harp from the scapula bone (or shoulder blade) of a cow or horse, with a carved bird holding a tricolour in its mouth perched on top of the harp at one end and his name (misspelt should have been MacSuibhne) carved on top of the other end. Housed in a glass display case, it also contains his wedding ring and empty bullet shells. This harp took pride of place in the family home in St. Patrick's Road but is now on display in the Limerick Museum.

Image of the harp carved by Johnny while interned in Ballykinlar which is on display in the Limerick Museum.

Three days after the signing of the Anglo-Irish Treaty, on 9 December 1921, all Republican prisoners were released from Ballykinlar. The immediate release of all political prisoners in Ballykinlar was also negotiated as part of the Treaty talks in London. Three special trains brought the men to Dublin, from

Internment in Ballykinlar

where the internees made their own way to their home counties but it appeared that their ordeal did not necessarily end there. It was reported in the *New York Times* on 9 December that;

> A trainload of released internees of the Ballykinlar Camp entered the station here this evening. Several bombs were exploded, injuring three of the released men, one of them seriously. Some persons in the crowd around the platform were slightly hurt by splinters". It is also documented that "the trains were attacked by loyalist mobs with gunfire, bricks and stones at several locations (25).

It would appear that Johnny returned to somewhat of a hero's welcome in Limerick upon his release. The *Limerick Leader* reported that Johnny's return, together with his brother Paddy and a J. Larkin (the three of which were described in a later article as a 'Trinity of heroes') attracted a large crowd to the railway station. Those present included the Deputy Mayor, members of the Corporation and representatives of the Sinn Féin executive, all of whom cordially welcomed the released prisoners. There was wild cheering as they walked from the platform and reached the terminus. Three city bands were present and paraded the streets (26).

Before their release, the prisoners put together a giant autograph book containing the names of all the prisoners known as the *Book of Ballykinlar*. This book, which is exhibited in the library of the Bureau of Military History in Rathmines, is richly illustrated with the names or signatures of prisoners arranged by geographical area and is a beautiful example of artwork from the internment camp. It has been argued 'that it must be one of the 'treasures' of Ireland such is its importance and uniqueness'.

OVERLEAF
A copy of one of the cover pages (left) and a Limerick page of signatures (right) from the Book of Ballykinlar with Johnny's, Denis's and Paddy's signature 4th, 5th & 6th up from the bottom respectively.

(Courtesy Military Archives ref. IE-MA-PRCN-0020-01-03)

The Forgotten Vice-Commandant

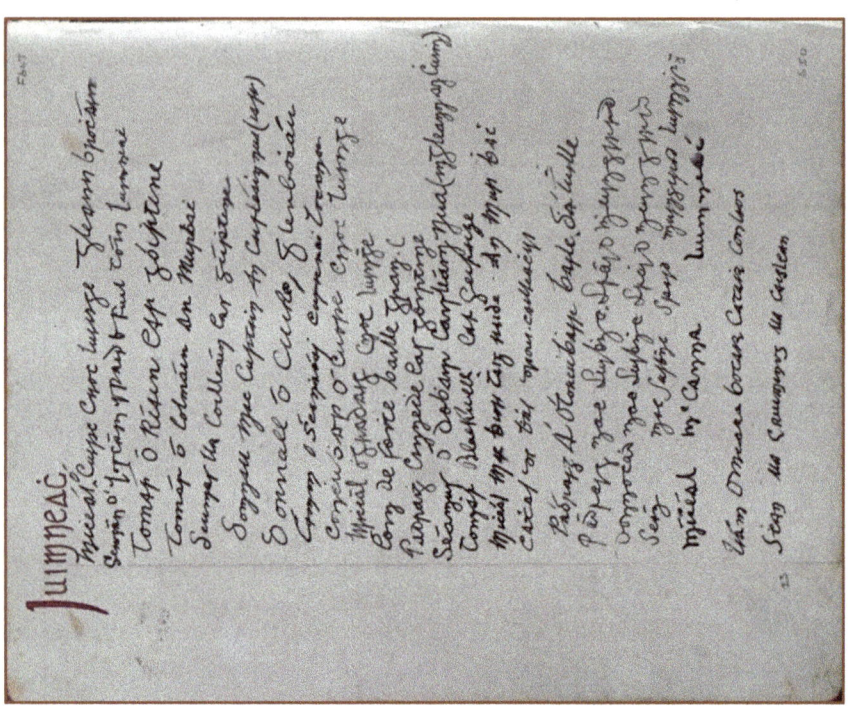

Internment in Ballykinlar

Photograph of image of Camp 1 from the Book of Ballykinlar. (Courtesy Military Archives, Ireland (IE-MA-PC-1050-01-01-01, from the Private Collection of Major General Hugo MacNeill). Captions by author.

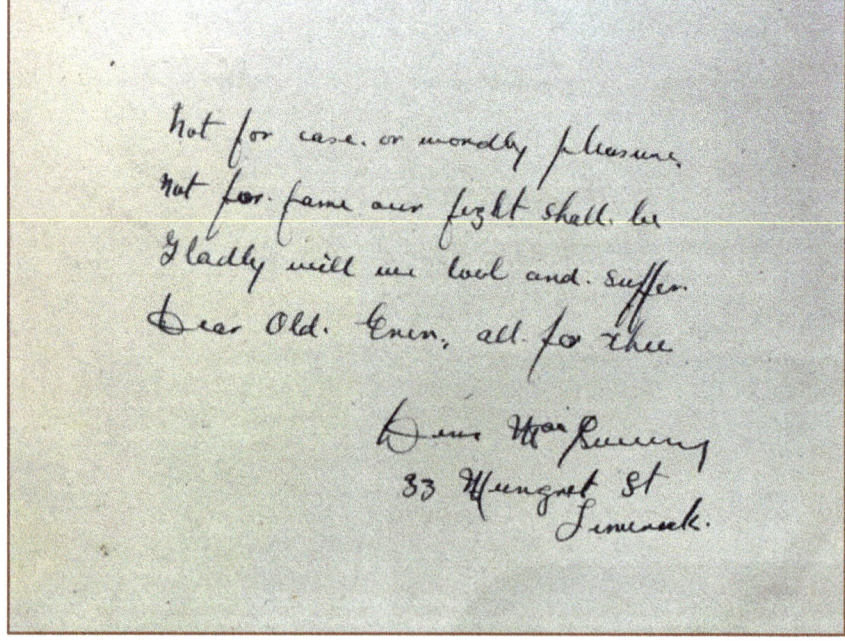

Entries made by Johnny (top) and Denis (bottom) in an autograph book owned by Pádraig Hannelly, from Castlerea who was interned in Hut 31.
(Image courtesy of Pádraig Hannelly's granddaughter Mary Ryan)

Chapter 9

The Civil War

After the signing of the Treaty and his subsequent release from Ballykinlar, Johnny took the Republican (anti-Treaty) side in the ensuing Civil War, which started on 28 June 1922. This was a war that was aptly described by Madge Daly as 'the saddest period in our history, the comrades of yesterday fighting and killing one another' (1). This bitter war was caused as a result of deep divisions created between pro- and anti-Treaty supporters. Those who favoured acceptance argued that the powers it granted made it worthy of support and would ultimately lead to an Irish Republic by accepting the principle that while it did not achieve the ultimate freedom that all nations desire it would give them the freedom to achieve it and the only alternative was renewed war with Britain. The Treaty's opponents criticised it most because of the requirement for elected deputies in Dáil Éireann having to swear allegiance to the king and its failure to achieve the status of a republic for a thirty-two county Ireland. In effect, they saw it as a desertion of the republic they had sworn to defend since it was proclaimed in 1916, and ratified by the first elected Dáil in 1919, thereby confining the country to dominion status within the British Commonwealth.

Johnny's decision to take the Republican side is reflected in the following account from an article written about him in later years by a fellow comrade who took a similar course of action.

> It was no easy matter for him to break with old friends because his heart was full of love for every sincere Irish man, but the moment he became convinced that it was his duty to strike out on a new line he did so, irrespective of what might be thought of his action (2).

The Civil War began in Dublin in June 1922 when those in favour of the Treaty, the Free State soldiers (or National Troops), under instructions from the British began shelling the Four Courts. This building was occupied since 13 April by 200 anti-Treaty republicans (often referred to as irregulars by their opponents), in an attempt to pressurise the provisional government of the Free State to reopen the war with Britain. The Free State soldiers captured the Four Courts on 30 June. Street fighting ensued in Dublin for a week until 5 July but then the attention turned to Munster. The province at that time was largely an anti-Treaty stronghold. The Republican forces' plan was to set up a 'Munster Republic' by creating a fortified defensive line between Waterford and Limerick. The hope was that in doing so, they would be in a position to renegotiate the Treaty.

Limerick was to become an important strategic location and both sides acknowledged that the control of Limerick city was fundamental to the outcome of the war (3). The leader of the Free State forces in the city at this time was East Clare Brigade Commander, Michael Brennan, who had distinguished himself during the War of Independence. Johnny knew him well as he was one of the six who along with Johnny voted in favour of proceeding with the Rising in Limerick at the Brigade meeting in 1916. Also, Johnny's brother, Paddy, was assigned, some ten years earlier, the role of vetting Michael Brennan before he was sworn into the IRB (4). An account suggests that Brennan only chose the Free State side due to an ongoing and bitter feud between him and his comrades in the Mid-Clare Brigade when he learned that those individuals chose the Republican side. It has also been suggested that this theory is evident from the fact that of the total of five executions of Republican prisoners carried out under his command during the Civil War, all five were from Brennan's own Mid-Clare Brigade (5). Indeed, as I will refer to later, two of these executions occurred in Limerick Prison at a time when Johnny was also imprisoned there.

Following the capture of the Four Courts and the end of the fighting in Dublin on 5 July, a state of heightened tension existed in the city between Brennan and the Republican forces Chief-of-Staff, Liam Lynch. Free State soldiers and anti-treaty soldiers occupied prominent buildings/ key positions in the city. At this time, the Republican forces had the upper hand as they had superior numbers and arms. Additionally, republicans were the more battle-hardened as their forces were made up of War of Independence veterans whereas the Free State army was largely made up of inexperienced recruits. However, Lynch, in a huge tactical miscalculation, agreed on a series of peace deals which held until 11 July. This delay in fighting benefited the pro-Treaty side as it allowed them time to gather forces and consolidate in the area (6). Following the British soldiers' withdrawal, republicans occupied the four military barracks in the city; The Strand Barracks (on what is now Clancy's Strand), the New Barracks (now known as Sarsfield Barracks), Castle Barracks (a barracks located inside the walls of King John's Castle) and the Ordnance Barracks (where the new Court House is located in Mulgrave Street). Johnny was stationed in the New (Sarsfield) Barracks. The Republicans also controlled the two bridges over the Shannon in the city. The pro-Treaty forces occupied William Street RIC (Police) Barracks and Cruises Hotel where Brennan set up his headquarters. They dug a trench across the road and worked their way, by breaking holes through the terraced georgian buildings, until they got to the Sarsfield Street side of the bridge where they set up a barricade. They built barricades across the entrance to O'Connell Street, William Street and Denmark Street, thereby creating a defensive ring around their headquarters. They also stationed snipers in the windows of the buildings of these streets.

On 11 July, events finally came to a head as the first shots were fired when two Free State soldiers, having been surprised by republicans in Roche's Street corner, offered resistance when attempts were being made to disarm and arrest them. It resulted in the shooting dead of one of the Free State soldiers (7). This incident was followed shortly afterwards by an attack on the Ordnance Barracks and low-intensity fighting broke out throughout the city where both sides continued to erect makeshift barricades. Republican forces largely held the ground to the south of the city and were able to rush in reinforcements to the New (Sarsfield) Barracks from North Cork and County Limerick as soon as the fighting started. The Free State soldiers had a supply line via Athlunkard Bridge to Clare and the rest of the country north of the Limerick-Waterford 'Munster Republic' line. William Street served as the Free State's front-line with buildings on each side of it held by opposing troops (8).

As noted earlier, Johnny was stationed in the New (Sarsfield) Barracks with the chief of staff of Republican forces Liam Lynch, who established this barracks as his headquarters. Indeed, I remember my father telling me that the kitchen table in our family

The Civil War

Barricades at the junction of O'Connell St. and Sarsfield St. (top) and Free State positions outside of Cruises Hotel. (*Top image courtesy of the George Imbusch photo archive. Bottom images courtesy of Limerick Museum. Colourising commissioned by author.*)

The Forgotten Vice-Commandant

home in St. Patrick's Road came from the Officers' Mess in this barracks. This barracks did not come under direct attack from the Free State forces because Lynch moved his headquarters to Clonmel. He realised how vulnerable his position was as the Free State army could capture his position in the barracks and end the Civil War in one fell swoop. They had, however, to deal with a sniper stationed on the church tower in St. Michael's Church in Barrington Street from where he commanded a perfect view of the barracks square where he inflicted many injuries on the Republican forces as they moved around the square (9).

Outside of the numerous smaller skirmishes that took place the major battles that did happen largely occurred within the city centre. The most notable of these was an attack by the republicans on the Free State troops holed up in the strategically-located Munster Fair Tavern in Mulgrave Street, which they captured and held briefly. The Free State troops responded swiftly by launching a successful counter-attack and re-took the building using armoured cars. They then proceeded to attack and mine the Ordnance Barracks which the republicans successfully defended against (10).

Free State soldiers eventually managed to secure three of the four bridges leading into Limerick city. Only Thomond Bridge was held by the Republican forces when attention turned to the retaking of the Strand Barracks. This attack turned out to be a major battle involving artillery fire. The commander of the Republican forces in this barracks was Captain Connie Mackey of C-Company of the Mid-Limerick Brigade, who is the subject of a book entitled *Not While I Have Ammo*. As noted earlier, Johnny is mentioned in this book as having sworn Connie Mackey into the IRB in 1917. An all-out attack was launched on Republican positions in both barracks on 15 July involving armoured cars, grenades, machine guns and mortar fire. This initial onslaught was successfully defended against; however, substantial Free State reinforcements came to Limerick by road and sea and included an eighteen-pounder artillery gun. This battle of Strand Barracks went on for five days until 20 July when the Republican forces, who had courageously defended the barracks until continuous artillery fire penetrated its walls. They were hopelessly outnumbered and forced to surrender.

The shelled-out Strand Barracks
(Courtesy Limerick Museum, colourising commissioned by author)

Upon hearing the artillery fire, other forces in the city tried to come to the aid of those in the Strand Barracks and attempted to break through the Free State lines. As a result, another fierce battle, including the use of grenades, ensued on O'Connell Street before the republicans were driven back by machine-gun fire from troops stationed at the northern (O'Connell Street) end of both Thomas Street and William Street (11). Once the Strand Barracks was captured, the Free State forces artillery fire was then aimed at the depleted forces in Castle Barracks (in King John's Castle) which

The Forgotten Vice-Commandant

they easily captured. The remaining Republican forces inside were rescued by boatmen who carried them across the River Shannon to safety (12). This effectively ended the battle for Limerick City and on the evening of 20 July, Liam Lynch issued an order to the remaining forces in the Ordnance and New Barracks to burn the two Barracks and retreat southwards. An account stated 'he (Lynch) must have realised the futility of opposing artillery in street fighting and he ordered the general withdrawal' (13).

Johnny and his comrades in the garrison that held the New Barracks immediately began dousing the inside of each building with petrol and paraffin, setting them on fire to deny the Free State enemies the use of a strategic building from which they could control the city. At 12:30 pm three huge mine explosions rocked the Military Road (now called Edward Street) entrance of the New Barracks, partially demolishing the gateway and blocking it with rubble (14). As they left the Barracks, the few remaining republicans covered the retreating forces with machine-gun fire, keeping the advancing Free State soldiers at bay. They had been attempting to encircle the barracks and trap the Republicans inside. From an account, it would appear at this stage a lot of the Limerick Republican forces simply went home (15). However, Johnny continued on with the remaining forces and retreated south towards Kilmallock. They only stopped briefly every few miles to fell trees across the roads, plant landmines and demolish bridges with explosives to slow any Free State troops advancing behind them (16).

OPPOSITE
Images over of the devastation caused by the Republican occupiers of the New (Sarsfield) Barracks in which Johnny took part before retreating southward to Buttevant. The barracks in flames (top). Free State soldier pointing to an unexploded mine in the barracks grounds (middle left). Free State soldiers in occupation of the burnt-out barracks (middle right and bottom). *(Photographs courtesy Limerick Museum)*

The Civil War

The Forgotten Vice-Commandant

OPPOSITE
Photographs showing panoramic images of the still smouldering barracks with civilian looting underway (top) and the burnt-out remnants (bottom). *(Images courtesy of the George Imbusch photo archive-colourising commissioned by author)*

A Republican soldier's account of this retreat states;

> And so we fell back through Patrickswell, Adare, finally ending up in Buttevant about 4 o'clock in the morning of 21st of July. We felt hopelessly disillusioned and disheartened. The whole flaming struggle seemed to be leading nowhere. They captured our men, held them and later shot some of them. We captured their men, sometimes twice over, and had to let them go. We had nowhere to put them, no arrangements. No one had a heart to fight [17].

There would also appear to have been an element of Cork Limerick rivalry in the ranks of the anti-Treaty IRA: an account stated that;

> We're the Limerick column... We're after fighting our way down from Patrickswell when we got here the Cork men had meat for breakfast and we had none. Tell (Deasy)–(the officer in charge of the 1st. southern division of the Republican's) if the Limerick men don't get meat there will be mutiny [18].

The retreating Republican troops took up a defensive position in Kilmallock with a force of 500 and another 1,000 further south in Buttevant [19]. That would explain Johnny's presence in Buttevant, where according to her pension application, Johnny's wife Kate stated that he collapsed there on 27 July 1922 [20]. Regarding the above comments in relation to general organisation and lack of supplies, his collapse must have been as a result of these factors which no doubt would have left him in a weakened state. Indeed, Michael Colivet his commanding officer confirmed as much when he recorded that;

The Civil War

During the Civil War, he really noticed that Johnny appeared haggard and worn and the tough times and rough food had a very bad effect on him. In Buttevant he was very bad, and we sent him back for hospital treatment (21).

From Buttevant he was taken to Cork North Infirmary Hospital where he remined from 27 July 1922 until 5 September 1922 when he was arrested by Free State troops (22). From here he was imprisoned in Limerick Prison (23). The circumstances surrounding his arrest are somewhat unclear. Kate states in her pension application that while being moved to Limerick on 6 September 1922, he was arrested by Free State forces and Liam Ford, one of his commanding officers, similarly records that he was arrested while being moved to a Limerick Hospital (24). Whereas Micheal Colivet, his commanding officer states that he was arrested out of the hospital and was allegedly ill-treated (25).

Meanwhile having lost a number of battles in Patrickswell, Adare, Newcastle West and a significant engagement in Kilmallock, Cork and Waterford quickly fell to Free State soldiers. The wife of Johnny's comrade, Michael Hartney who was a member of the Cumann na mBan, was killed during a battle that the retreating forces fought in Adare. From this time forward, the Civil War reverted to a guerrilla war.

Conditions in Limerick Prison at the time of Johnny's capture and imprisonment there were horrendous. The prison, designed to hold 120 prisoners, swelled by captured Republican soldiers, contained up to 700 by November (26). Extracts from a report on the prison's conditions prepared around this time stated;

> This place is overcrowded and the conditions under which we are compelled to live are something appalling. Inferior food, no beds or blankets for the greater number of men. I was refused a business visit yesterday. Four boys here collapsed and have been moved into the

> prison hospital. One lad J.J. Tierney, is unconscious and his mother was refused a visit………..From another prisoner, we learn that cells intended for one, now contain eight men. Many of the prisoners have not even a blanket, the bed clothing supplied is filthy: there is no underclothing of any kind: there are no medical arrangements and no baths: no adequate cooking arrangements. Some prisoners do not get breakfast until 2 PM. No visits are allowed. On August 30, when about 30 of the prisoners were going to bed, about a dozen shots were fired down the corridors by order of Captain Shaugnessy (sic). Shots are continually been fired from the tower of the gaol towards the relatives of the prisoners who come to the walls. (27)

Madge Daly actively canvassed for improved conditions for the prisoners and in a letter to the Mayor of Limerick in October 1922 (less than one month after Johnny's imprisonment there) she wrote;

> Things have become infinitely worse …. The sick list is increasing daily over 80% of the prisoners are now suffering from infections, skin disease particularly scabies. Four baths for 700 prisoners. And nothing is being done to alleviate (28).

Two Republican prisoners from County Clare were also executed by firing squad in the prison during Johnny's period of detention. Another prisoner was shot dead by a Free State soldier guarding him at the time for making hand signals to another prisoner (29).

In addition to the overcrowding and unsanitary conditions, incidents of brutality and intimidation also occurred within the jail. Constance Markievicz, who visited Limerick at this time, reported conditions in the prison in a letter to the editor of *Freedom* where, in addition to highlighting particular instances of beatings of Republican prisoners in an effort to extract information, she stated;

> Another boy who escaped from the jail told me that the cells were constantly fired into, and the night before he got out a bullet struck the floor where he was sleeping on between his head and that of his comrade (30).

The Forgotten Vice-Commandant

Johnny's continuing ill health, having already been weakened by his collapse in Buttevant, was no doubt easy prey to these appalling conditions. Until finally, on 22 January 1923, after nearly four-and-a-half months imprisonment he was ordered by a doctor to the City Home Hospital in Limerick (31) where he remained until he died from consumption of the bowels (or TB as it was more commonly known) on 10 April 1923 (32). He died somewhat ironically on the very day that according to historian Tom Mahon, the Irish Civil War, 'effectively ended,' when the Free State army fatally wounded IRA Chief of Staff Liam Lynch during a skirmish in County Tipperary. Lynch had left Limerick and set up his headquarters in Clonmel. Twenty days later, on 30 April 1923, a ceasefire order was given. Following this, on 24 May 1923, the Civil War officially ended when Lynch's successor Frank Aiken, gave the order to 'Surrender and dump arms' (33).

At the time of his death, Johnny's brother, Paddy, was also detained in Limerick Prison and was refused permission for temporary release to attend his funeral. Instead, the wardens allowed Paddy access to the roof of the prison where he could view his older brother's funeral cortege as it passed Limerick Prison making its way to Mount St. Lawrence Cemetery (34).

As with the War of Independence, I have not come across any documented accounts of specific activities that Johnny was involved in the Civil War while stationed in the New Barracks or later on in the retreat southwards towards Cork. Again, I do not think it would be conjecturing to assume, given his senior level of involvement in both the planned insurrection in 1916 and the War of Independence activities in Limerick, that he was involved at some senior level with the planning and implementation of activities in the Civil War in Limerick City. He was stationed with the leader of the Republican forces in the New Barracks and at that stage he was Vice-Commandant of the 2nd Battalion of the Mid-Limerick Brigade. Furthermore, given the intense fighting and smaller skirmishes that took place over the ten-day period in the battle for Limerick, it would have been virtually impossible for him to have had no involvement.

Although I have no information on any specific incidents with which Johnny was involved, it is documented that his activities did come to the attention of senior officers in the Free State Army. As is evident in a report from the Adjutant of the Southern command dated 19 September 1924 (35), which stated that Johnny took an active part in the operations in the Civil War, particularly at Limerick. Owing to failing health, however, he was a patient in the North Charitable and County Infirmary Cork. In addition, the report goes on to state that 'while he was detained in Cork he was all the time however keeping in touch with the Irregulars and was subsequently arrested by National Troops and removed to the County Jail Limerick'. Liam Ford recorded that 'Johnny was one of the most active members of the Brigade' (36).

By way of an interesting anecdote to this chapter. The extent of Civil War divisions is particularly evident in a document from the pension application of Johnny's comrade Michael Hartney which he completed years later in 1935. When in a response to a standard question on the application form 'Did you serve in the national army' he answered somewhat frankly 'Never thank God'. Whilst I was struck by what would today appear to be a somewhat humorous reply, it was never intended this way. Hartney would have written this reply because he genuinely felt it and in addition, he would have done so in the full knowledge that this statement could impact negatively on the assessment of his pension application.

Chapter 10

The Republican Plot

Johnny is interred in the Republican Plot in Mount St. Lawrence Cemetery along with a number of his comrades mentioned earlier. They include Seoirse Clancy and Michael O'Callaghan, the Mayor and former Mayor of Limerick respectively, who were shot dead at home on the same night by the Black and Tans (Clancy's Strand and O'Callaghan's Strand are named in their memory). Johnny is pictured with Seoirse Clancy in the image in Chapter Three. Another Volunteer, Joseph O'Donoghue was also murdered that night and the trio's assassinations became known as the Curfew Murders. They were the first burials to take place in the Republican Plot.

It was always the intention to mark these Republican graves in an appropriate manner, but it was not until March 1934 that the twenty-two foot, ten-inches high limestone Celtic cross memorial and the enclosing limestone plinth was erected following the efforts of a fundraising committee. Madge Daly who was a trustee of the plot played a large role in this effort (1). The cross was designed by Oliver Sheppard RHA, a noted Irish sculptor who is best known for

The Republican Plot

his bronze sculpture the *Death of Cuchulainn* located in the GPO in Dublin which commemorates the Rising. Patrick Pearse's brother, Willie, who was also executed for his part in the Rising, was a student of his. The cross was sculpted locally by stonemasons from the Pike, Messers Keane Monumental Sculptors, owned by Bill Keane who along with his two sons were members of A-Company of the 2nd Battalion (2). An account states that the fundraising committee set out to raise in the region of £1,000 for the cross, and a large list of subscribers who were from different political creeds was listed in the *Limerick Leader* at the time. The Mc Sweeney Family, Mungret St. was listed as subscribing, a not-insubstantial amount (at that time), of £5.00 which would have been one of the larger donations listed (3). The blessing of the cross was attended by 2,000 people on 18 March 1934 in what was described as an impressive ceremony that included prominent citizens and a choir of over 100 singers. Johnny's wife, Kate, and his brother, Paddy, were listed in a *Limerick Leader* article as amongst the relatives attending (4).

The translation of the Irish inscription on the cross reads '*A prayer for the 19 who died for the Republic of Ireland*'. Johnny was the last of the original nineteen to be buried in the plot until the burial of Sean South some thirty-four years later in 1957. This was followed by the burial of the widows of the murdered ex-mayor and mayor in 1961 and 1962 respectively. The last burial, in 1968, was that of the wife of executed IRA Captain Thomas Keane. Madge Daly was one of only three trustees of the plot and she makes an interesting recollection in her witness statement concerning burials in the plot.

> I was Trustee for the Republican Burial Plot. The other Trustees were both on the Free State side. I had the Plot opened for the burial of all republicans killed in the Civil War and the Free State

The Forgotten Vice-Commandant

An early photograph of the plot (circa April/ May 1922) at which time there were only nine interred. From left Michael O'Callaghan (plot 5), George Clancy (plot 6), Joseph O'Donoghue (plot 7). The three killed the night of the curfew murders - Henry Clancy (plot 8), Seán Wall (plot 9), James Horan (plot 10), Tadgh Hennessy (plot 11) and Thomas Keane (plot 12). Patrick Downey remains (plot 16) were also interred there at this time, but his plot appears unmarked in this photograph (see diagram on page 111 for plot references).

Photograph of a section of the attendance at the official unveiling/ blessing of the cross.   *(Images courtesy of Des Long, captured by his father David RIP)*

> Trustees never made an effort to stop me, or to have Free State soldiers buried there - an admission that they had no right to do so, having deserted the Republic they had sworn to defend (5).

The final resting place of Johnny is, perhaps, best epitomised in the final paragraph of an obituary written by a former comrade of his, Michael Hartney, Captain of E-Company of the 2nd Battalion, with whom he was interned in Wormwood Scrubs. As mentioned earlier Hartney's wife was a member of Cumann na mBan and was killed in Adare during the Civil War. She is also buried in the Republican Plot (in the grave next to Johnny's).

> Johnny's remains rest in the company of those of Ireland's best in the Republican Plot in Mount St. Lawrence Cemetery. Surrounding him are the bodies of those he loved because they loved Ireland. He rests there as a result of wearing himself out in the service of Dark Rosaleen, and with its other occupants, he prays round the Great White Throne for Ireland and Ireland's best (6).

Of the original nineteen buried in this plot, nine were killed in the War of Independence and ten during the Civil War all of which were from the Republican side. It is also important to note that the plot was only opened late in the War of Independence. As a result, there were a number of Volunteers who died during this period who are not buried in this plot. In all, there are a total of twenty-three buried there.

Brief account of those interred in the Republican Plot

Although I have referenced the plots in numerical order in the diagram over, I have done so based on their location only as the sequence of burials did not follow any orderly pattern within the plot itself. The following accounts are set out in chronological order as it helps to better understand the circumstances surrounding the deaths of each individual interred here. Thus, the plot numbers are used solely for referencing with the diagram and bear no relevance as to the order of burials.

> Please note that the following information is compiled based on the best possible interpretation of available documentation. Regard needs to be taken for the fact that published information about those interred here, in particular, the circumstances surrounding the deaths during the Civil War period is difficult to conclusively verify as misinformation was put out by both sides of the conflict. In some cases, varying accounts are given. In addition, there was a lack of published information in the local newspapers. The *Limerick Leader* and *Limerick Chronicle*, did not publish for a period of time during the fall of Limerick. Also, my research was carried out before the recent refurbishment of the plot and in some cases, the names and dates of death were either worn off or illegible on the gravemarkers. Therefore I have had to rely on previously documented sources of information on the Republican Plot. In this regard, I have established in three cases that the dates of death vary somewhat from these earlier sources. In addition, in one case the date given on a legible grave marker was incorrect. However, in all cases, I have set out the basis of my conclusions on the footnotes accompanying each plot's description. I made my research available to Des Long of the Limerick Republican Graves prior to the recent refurbishment of the plot and these new dates have been used in the re-engraving of the grave markers.

The Republican Plot

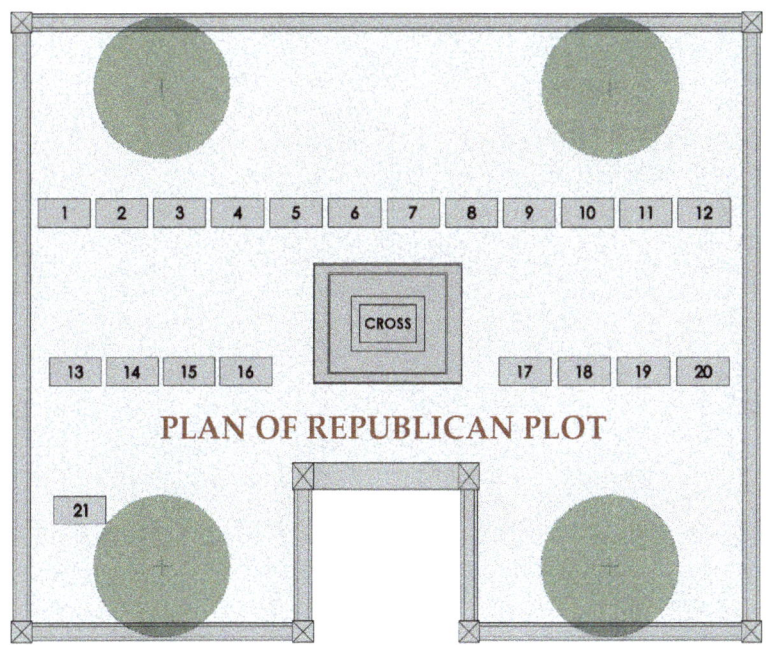

PLAN OF REPUBLICAN PLOT

PLOT NO.1
Michael Danford
Captain
Died 28-8-1922*

PLOT NO. 2
John Hogan
Volunteer
Died 13-8-1922

PLOT NO. 3
Denis O'Dwyer
Volunteer, Died 7-8-1922

PLOT NO. 4
Kate O'Callaghan
(The Murdered ex Mayor's wife)
Died 16-3-1961

PLOT NO. 5
Michael O'Callaghan
Mayor of Limerick 1920
Died 7-3-1921

PLOT NO. 6
George Clancy
Mayor of Limerick
Vice-Commandant Mid-Limerick
Brigade
Died 7-3-1921
And his wife, Maire
Died 8-6-1962

PLOT NO. 7
Joseph O'Donoghue
Volunteer, Died 7-3-1921

PLOT NO. 8
Henry Clancy
Volunteer
Died 1-5-1921

PLOT NO. 9
Sean Wall
Brigade Commandant,
East Limerick Brigade
Died 6-5-1921

PLOT NO. 10
James Horan
Captain
Died 1-5-1921

PLOT NO. 11
Tadgh Hennessy
Lieutenant
Died 17-5-1921

PLOT NO. 12
Thomas Keane
Captain
Died 4-6-1921
And Helen Keane
Died 22-2-1968

PLOT NO. 13
Owen O'Brien
Brigade Vice-Commandant
Died 30-3-1923

PLOT NO. 14
Tadhg Hayes
Volunteer, Died 13-8-1922

PLOT NO. 15
Edward O'Dwyer
Section-Commander
Died 7-8-1922

PLOT NO. 16
Patrick (also known as Michael)
Downey
Section-Commander
Died 4-5-1921*

PLOT NO. 17
Mrs Margaret Hartney
Cumann na mBan
Died 4-8-1922

PLOT NO. 18
John Mc Sweeney
Battalion Vice-Commandant
Died 10-4-1923

PLOT NO. 19
Henry Meany
Died 2-8-1922
Staff Captain (Battalion
Commandant)

PLOT NO. 20
Patrick Naughton
Captain
Died 25-7-1922

PLOT NO, 21
Sean South
Volunteer
Died 1-1-1957

A historic photograph of The Republican Plot circa the early 1950s from the Daly Papers *(Courtesy of the Special Collections and Archives, University of Limerick)*

Johnny's grave marker in Mount St. Lawrence's Burial Ground (plot reference Ka 196). English translation reads; John Mc Sweeney, Vice-Commandant, died 10th April 1923

PLOT NO. 7
Joseph O'Donoghue
Volunteer
Died 7-3-1921

Volunteer O'Donoghue, aged twenty-four, was a loyal and active member of E-Company, 2nd Battalion Mid-Limerick Brigade. Originally from Rathduff, Ballynacargy, county Westmeath, he was employed as a manager in the River Plate Meat Company in William Street and was well-known in the GAA and gaelic league circles. Between 11:30 and 12.00 on the night of the sixth, shortly after saying the rosary and retiring for the night, a party of masked and armed Crown forces called to his house in Janesboro. His room was searched and he was taken away and murdered. His bullet-ridden body was found the next day some distance away from his home. This was the first murder of, what became known as, the Curfew Murders to occur that night (7).

PLOT NO. 5
Michael O'Callaghan
Mayor of Limerick 1920
Died 7-3-1921

O'Callaghan, aged forty-one, from North Strand, Limerick (renamed O'Callaghan Strand in his honour). Murdered in his home in what was the second of the Curfew Murders. O'Callaghan was present at the first meeting to establish the Irish Volunteers in Limerick where he spoke on the platform with Patrick Pearse and Roger Casement. He was on the Executive Committee of the Irish Volunteers from 1914 to 1916. Elected Mayor of Limerick in 1920 and was described by his wife 'as the brains of Sinn Féin in Limerick a fact known to those who planned and paid for his murder' (8).

PLOT NO. 6
George (Seoirse) Clancy
Mayor of Limerick
Vice-Commandant Mid-Limerick Brigade
Died 7-3-1921
And his wife, Maire
Died 8-6-1962

Commandant Clancy, age thirty-eight, Castleview Gardens, Thomondgate (originally from Grange, Co. Limerick). Clancy's Strand was renamed in his honour. Vice-Commandant, Mid-Limerick Brigade. He was an active Volunteer and a former head centre of the IRB in Limerick who was executed by Crown forces while Mayor of Limerick in his home in what was the third of the Curfew Murders. Described by his wife as 'A nationalist who drank in the tenets of militant Irish Nationality from an early age, a Gaelic Leaguer before the Gaelic League and a Sinn Feiner before Sinn Féin'. One of his friends at university was the writer James Joyce, who based the character Davin, the young nationalist and 'peasant scholar,' in his book *Portrait of the Artist as a Young Man*. His wife, Maire, a founder member of Cumann na mBan, who is also interred in this plot, witnessed her husband's shooting in the hallway of her home where she sustained a bullet wound to her wrist (9).

The remains of O'Donoghue, O'Callaghan and Clancy were the first burials in the Republican Plot. The following extract from an Irish Press article dated the seventh of March 1932 poignantly reflected on these events.

> These three crimes were no haphazard attack, but a pre-concerted assault on the three strongest bulwarks of Irish nationhood - on Gaelic Ireland personified by Seoirse Clancy; on industrial Ireland in Michael O'Callaghan; and on young Ireland in the person of Joseph O'Donoghue.

PLOT NO. 8
Henry Clancy
Volunteer
Died 1-5-1921

Volunteer Clancy, age twenty-one, of 4 Garvey's Range, Limerick, Company officer (Section Leader), C-Company, 2nd Battalion, Mid-Limerick Brigade and a member of the Mid-Limerick Brigade Active Service Unit. He was one of a group of three Volunteers that were meeting to exchange guns in a field near Ballysimon Road Railway Bridge when they were surprised by a patrol of RIC and Black and Tans. One of the Volunteers took flight and escaped, but Clancy and his comrade Thomas Keane hid thinking they were not seen. But they were spotted and captured. Clancy thought he had managed to distract one of his captors and made a bid to escape but had only got twenty or thirty yards when the RIC and Black and Tans opened fire and fatally wounded him. It was reported by Crown forces that the men were preparing for an ambush at Singland Railway Bridge and fired on the RIC, and fled across fields. In the ensuing battle, Clancy was shot dead. A memorial marking the area where he was shot is located on the Ballysimon Road near the railway bridge. Clancy's accomplice, comrade and friend, Volunteer Thomas Keane was captured alive but later executed (see plot 12). Clancy was unmarried and worked as a railway labourer (10).

PLOT NO. 10
James Horan
Captain
Died 1-5-1921

Captain Horan, aged thirty-two, from Caherconlish, A-Company, 4th Battalion, Mid-Limerick Brigade and a member of the Mid-Limerick Brigade Active Service Unit. Described as an outstanding soldier, he was killed when a mixed force of British military and police surprised the IRA in the act of setting up an ambush at Shraherla (between Kilfinnane and Kildorrery). The military laid down a withering fire from rifles and machine guns as the Volunteers retreated. James Horan and three of his comrades Patrick Casey, Timothy Hennessey and Patrick Starr from Nenagh facilitated the escape of their comrades by taking up positions and returning covering fire. James Horan and Patrick Starr were killed almost immediately. Timothy (Tadgh) Hennessey was wounded and died two weeks later (see Plot 11) (11).

PLOT NO. 16
Patrick (also known as Michael) Downey
Section-Commander
Died 4-5-1921*

Volunteer Downey aged twenty-eight, B-Company, 2nd Battalion, Mid-Limerick Brigade and a member of the Mid-Limerick Brigade Active Service Unit, from Rhebogue, Singland, Limerick. He was shot dead on St. Patrick's Hill during the War of Independence by Crown forces who gave chase to, and fired upon, a small group of Volunteers attempting to bypass a cordon of Crown forces that were seeking to break up the funeral cortege of those attending the burial of Volunteer Henry Clancy (see plot 8). A memorial marking the location of his shooting is erected on the side wall of St. Patrick's Well. Clancy's comrade, Gerald Noonan, was also shot and left for dead during this incident and he was removed along with Clancy to the morgue in the New Barracks and was only discovered to have survived when his groans were heard coming from the morgue during the night (12).

*Original grave marker incorrectly stated the fourth of July.

PLOT NO. 9
Sean Wall
Chairman Limerick County Council
Brigade Commandant, East Limerick Brigade
Died 6-5-1921

Commandant Wall aged thirty-two, Commandant East Limerick Brigade from Bruff. Founder member of the Bruff Company, was one of the more significant commanders in the region. The brigade in which he commanded was involved in a wide range of military engagements, ranking his flying column amongst the premier fighting units of the IRA. He was Chairman of Limerick County Council. On his way to a divisional council meeting, he and his staff were attacked by a RIC raiding party in a house near Annacarty, County Tipperary. In the ensuing fight, he was isolated and captured. His escort was then attacked by an IRA column during which one RIC sergeant was killed. His captors were forced to retreat but before doing so, they opened fire on Wall and killed him. Survived by his wife and five young children (13).

PLOT NO. 11
Tadgh Hennessy
Lieutenant
Died 17-5-1921

Volunteer Hennessey, aged twenty-six, F-Company, 4th Battalion, Mid-Limerick Brigade and a member of the Mid-Limerick Brigade Active Service Unit, from Killonan (originally from Ballybricken). Died following injuries received in the previously-mentioned ambush at Shraherla (see plot 10) when, after the shooting of two of their comrades, Hennessey and Patrick Casey reached a field between the church and the school. Here Hennessy was wounded and taken prisoner along with Casey, who at this stage, had an empty magazine in his gun had no choice but to surrender.

Hennessy died from his wounds in Cork under military detention two weeks later. Casey was court-martialled and sentenced to death by firing squad which was carried out in Cork within twenty-five hours of his capture (14).

PLOT NO. 12
Thomas Keane
Captain
Died 4-6-1921
And Helen Keane
Died 22-2-1968

Captain Keane aged thirty-four, C-Company, 2nd Battalion Mid-Limerick Brigade of 1 Moore Lane, Leila Street, Limerick. He was a railway worker and was married with two young children. He was executed by Crown forces in Limerick Detention Barracks in the New (Sarsfield) Barracks by firing squad after being convicted of levying war and possession of arms following his capture in Singland where his comrade and friend Henry Clancy was shot dead (see plot 8). He was initially buried inside Sarsfield Barracks but following the Treaty his remains were removed from the grave in the barracks on 7 April 1922 and interred in the Republican Plot. He was the only Volunteer to be executed by Crown forces in the War of Independence outside of Dublin and Cork. A memorial is erected in Sarsfield Barracks to his memory. Before his execution, his wife Helen, who is also buried in this plot and was pregnant at this time, assembled outside the barracks with her mother and large crowds to pray for the repose of her husband's soul. She was attacked by a RIC Sergeant, who made an onslaught with his baton on the assembled crowd who were kneeled in prayer (15).

Keane was the last to be interred in this plot from the War of Independence period as he was sadly executed just over a month before the Truce on 11 July 1921 which ended the conflict.

PLOT NO. 20
Patrick Naughton
Captain
Died 25-7-1922

Captain Naughton aged twenty-five, of 1 Keefe's Place (or lane), Edward Street, Limerick, F-Company 2nd Battalion, Mid-Limerick Brigade. Transferred to West-Limerick Brigade area in April 1920 and joined the Brigade Active Service Unit. He took part in many attacks on the British Forces in Limerick including shooting dead a British soldier in the Railway Bar, Parnell Street during the War of Independence. He also saw action in the Civil War on the Republican side. He was shot in the City Mills, Roches Street, on 20 July during the battle for Limerick City in the Civil War and died five days later from his injuries. He was unmarried and worked in Bannatyne's Mill in the city (16).

PLOT NO. 19
Henry Meany
Died 2-8-1922
Staff Captain (Battalion Commandant)

Commandant Meany, John Street, Limerick, aged thirty-seven of C-Company 2nd Battalion Mid-Limerick Brigade and Brigade Intelligence Officer. A long-term member and early pioneer of the Volunteer movement in Limerick, he was imprisoned for political offences on a number of occasions during the War of Independence. During one of these periods of imprisonment in 1919, he took part in the hunger strike led by Robert Byrne which was the start of the series of events that culminated in the famous Limerick Soviet. Whilst remaining manacled and handcuffed, he was so weakened by this hunger strike that the Prison Governor, fearing he would die, sent for his family. He was a former president of the ITGWU and GWU trade unions and a member of the Munster Council of the GAA. He gave the order for the successful Republican attack on Patrickswell during the Civil War but was subsequently killed in the battle (17).

PLOT NO. 17
Mrs Margaret Hartney
Cumann na mBan
Died 4-8-1922

Aged thirty-five and an active Cumann na mBan member. Margaret Hartney was killed during the Civil War attending injured republicans, one of which included her husband. She was crossing a yard in the Dunraven Hotel in Adare which was made into a temporary hospital when a free State shell struck the hotel. Her husband Captain Michael Hartney of E-Company, a distinguished Volunteer, who was also badly wounded in Adare later highlighted that the shell was fired at the hotel even though it had a Red Cross flag flying over it. She was described by Madge Daly as 'a fine woman with a definite Fenian outlook who was a great worker'. In 1920 during the War of Independence, her shop and dwelling house in Davis Street were blown up by a landmine planted by the RIC. She was survived by her husband and two young daughters (18).

PLOT NO. 3
Denis O'Dwyer
Volunteer
7-8-1922

Volunteer O'Dwyer, aged twenty-three, F-Company, 2nd Battalion Mid-Limerick Brigade, Edward Street, Limerick. He was arrested along with two others near Rathkeale by Free State soldiers during the Civil War. After their arrest, they were fired upon by their captors where O'Dwyer was instantly killed and the other two wounded. One of the wounded was John Hogan who later died from his injuries (see plot no 2). His brother Edward was also killed on the same date just two hours apart (see plot 15) (19).

PLOT NO. 15
Edward O'Dwyer
Section-Commander
Died 7-8-1922

Volunteer O'Dwyer, aged twenty, F-Company, 2nd Battalion Mid-Limerick Brigade and a member of the Mid-Limerick Brigade Active Service Unit, from Edward Street, Limerick. Arrested in 1920, during the War of Independence, at the young age of seventeen and was sentenced to two years hard labour. He was the younger of the two brothers who died within two hours of each other in Newcastle West during the Civil War (see plot 3) (20).

PLOT NO. 2
John Hogan
Volunteer
Died 13-8-1922

Volunteer Hogan aged nineteen, D-Company, 2nd Battalion Mid-Limerick Brigade from 2 New Road, Thomongate was shot and injured in action in Newcastle West, along with Denis O'Dwyer who was fatally wounded (see plot 3), fighting for the Republican side during the Civil War and died from his injuries seven days later. Unmarried and worked as a labourer (21).

PLOT NO. 14
Tadhg Hayes
Volunteer
Died 13-8-1922

Volunteer Hayes, D-Company, 2nd Battalion Mid-Limerick Brigade, aged twenty, from 7 Lower Hartstonge Street, Limerick. Unmarried and worked as an assistant chemist with M. Mahon's in 8 William Street. He died in St John's Hospital, from the effects of a gunshot wound accidentally received by him on 4th July 1922 at the Telephone Exchange, Limerick during the IRA occupation of that building during the Civil War where he was serving as a battalion chemist (22).

PLOT NO.1
Michael Danford
Captain
Died 28-8-1922*

Captain Danford, aged twenty-six, D-Company, 2nd Battalion, Mid-Limerick Brigade and a member of the Mid-Limerick Brigade Active Service Unit, 1 Old Dominic St., Kings Island. He took part in many attacks on the British Forces in Limerick during the War of Independence including the failed rescue attempt of Robert Byrne from the City Home and he also commanded an attack on Crown forces at Sarsfield Street. He took the Republican side in the Civil War. He was arrested at his cousin's house on the Roxboro Road by three or four Free State army officers who took him to the brickworks at Clino on the Ballysimon Road where his bullet-ridden body was found the following morning. There is a roadside memorial at the location where his body was found to the left of the entrance to Crossagalla Business Park. He was married with four children, the youngest was only eight weeks old at the time of his death and he worked as gas a worker (lamplighter) (23).

*Grave marker states the twenty-eighth but death certificate submitted as part of family pension records states the twenty-ninth.

PLOT NO. 13
Owen O'Brien
Brigade Vice-Commandant
Died 30-3-1923

Commandant O'Brien, age thirty, Ballyvara, Lisnagry, Co. Limerick, originally from Bruff. Vice-Commandant Mid-Limerick Brigade at the end of the War of Independence. Originally Ahane Company, 3rd Battalion Mid-Limerick Brigade where he was in command in numerous actions such as the burning of Ballysimon Barracks, Mountshannon House and the blowing up of Annacotty Bridge during the War of Independence. He took the Republican side in the Civil War and died in Curragh Camp (Tintown) County Kildare where he was imprisoned since his capture in the Annacotty area on 9 September the previous year (24).

PLOT NO. 18
John Mc Sweeney
Battalion Vice-Commandant
Died 10-4-1923

Commandant Mc Sweeney aged forty-two, Vice-Commandant, 2nd Battalion, Mid-Limerick Brigade from Mungret Street, Limerick. Head centre of a Limerick Circle of the IRB and co-opted by the IRB onto the founding committee of the Irish Volunteers in Limerick. One of the six who were outvoted by ten-six at the brigade meeting to determine whether to proceed with the planned 1916 Easter insurrection in Limerick following MacNeil's countermanding order. He was also one of the founding members of the 2nd Battalion following the split in the 1st Battalion after the Rising. He was interned during the War of Independence in Wormwood Scrubs where he took part in the hunger strikes and was later interned in Ballykinlar Internment Camp. Took the Republican side in the Civil War and was stationed in the New (Sarsfield) Barracks during the battle for Limerick City. Died from the illness he contracted in the latter stages of the Civil War while imprisoned in the overcrowded and unsanitary conditions of Limerick Prison following his capture in Cork in September 1922. A brush maker by profession he was survived by his wife and six young children.

Johnny's was the last burial to take place during the War of Independence/ Civil War period.

**PLOT NO, 21
Sean South
Volunteer
Died 1-1-1957**

Seán South from Henry Street, Limerick was a member of an IRA military column who took part in a raid on an RUC Barracks in Brookeborough, County Fermanagh, on New Year's Day, 1957. This attack occurred during what became known as the border campaign. South died of wounds sustained during the attack along with another IRA Volunteer, Fergal O'Hanlon. The attack on the barracks inspired the well-known rebel song *Seán South of Garryowen*.

**PLOT NO. 4
Kate O'Callaghan
(The Murdered ex Mayor's wife)
Died 16-3-1961**

The widow of Michael O'Callaghan, former Mayor of Limerick, who was killed in her presence by Crown forces (see plot 5). She was a founding member of Cumann na mBan and served as local branch president for one year in 1921, was elected as a Sinn Féin TD in the 1921 elections and re-elected in 1922 as an anti-Treaty TD. She was imprisoned in harsh conditions in Kilmainham Jail during the Civil War where she took part in a hunger strike (25).

Maire Clancy
Died 8-6-1962

Interred with her husband George, see plot 6.

Helen Keane
Died 22-2-1968

Interred with her husband Thomas, see plot 12

CHAPTER 11

FAMILY LIFE

Life cannot have been easy for Johnny's wife Kate during this time, particularly during his periods of internment. In addition to not being allowed to visit him, she would have also had the uncertainty of not knowing at the time how long each period of internment was likely to last. She also gave birth after a period of illness to her youngest son Robert (Bertie) when Johnny was on hunger strike in Wormwood Scrubs. Although he was granted temporary parole for a short period from his internment to look after her, he still voluntarily returned to recommence his hunger strike shortly after the birth. Furthermore, when Johnny walked out the door on Easter Sunday morning 1916 she must have been beside herself with worry. In addition to wondering if she would ever see him alive again, she also had the additional worry of his ill health due to his refusal to go ahead with an operation. All this was at a time when she was in the latter stages of pregnancy with my father Roger, who was born five days later.

Also, financially they must have been tough times for her as she was at home with six young children with no obvious means of income and was reliant on agencies for support. At the time of

Johnny's death, her six children ranged in age from one month to nine years old. She received three pounds per week from the Prisoners Defence Fund and ten shillings per week for each child from the Orphan's Committee of the Irish White Cross (1). Johnny's income as a brush maker at that time would have been five pounds a week (2). After Johnny's death, she also made an application for a State pension which was payable at that time to Volunteers who died in the course of the conflict. In her application, she stated that Johnny never recovered from illnesses he received as a result of his hunger strike in Wormwood Scrubs (3). She made three such applications, but all were refused on the basis that his 'death did not occur as the result of specific wounds or injuries received in the course of duty' (4). In an appeal of her third refused application, she was finally successful and in 1935 she was granted this pension (5). It would appear that the reason for her successful appeal was as a result of the 1934 Military Service Pensions Act which was introduced so that those who had not applied, or were refused, under the 1924 Act could apply again. The main reason for the 1934 Act was because the majority of those who had supported the anti-Treaty side were either refused a pension by the Free State government or did not apply for one. It was not until 1932 when de Valera and the new Fianna Fáil government got into power did the anti-Treaty veterans feel they would get a fair hearing (6). Some financial assistance also came from other sources, as 'a benefit night' was funded to aid his family by the County Board of the GAA in 1924 in recognition of Johnny's interest in and service to the GAA (7).

Kate moved from Mungret Street with her young family to St. Patrick's Road in circa 1928 in a house she obtained with assistance from the Irish White Cross* where she resided until her death in February 1976 (8). Interestingly, she named this house 'Rosaville' a similar name to 'Roseville' which was the name of Bat Laffan's farm in Killonan where the Volunteers used to drill (9). It was clear that Kate must have mourned greatly after Johnny's death as I always have a recollection of her wearing black right up to the time of her death. She placed the following anniversary notice in the Limerick Leader in 1961 some 38 years after his death (10).

> **McSweeney (38th Anniversary)**
> In proud remembrance of my dear husband, John (Johnny) McSweeney (Vice-Commandant, 2nd. Batt., Mid Limerick Brigade, IRA), died April 10, 1923. RIP. May Jesus have mercy on him, masses offered.
> Thirty eight years. How long it seems
> Since that sad day you passed away
> And was buried in the Republican Plot next day
> Like falling leaves the years pass by,
> But memories of you, dear Johnny will never die
> -Always remember by his widow, daughter and sons

* The Irish White Cross was established on 1 February 1921, at the suggestion of Maud Gonne as a mechanism for distributing funds raised by the American Committee for Relief in Ireland with the intention of giving financial assistance to civilians in Ireland who had been injured or suffered severe financial hardship due to the ongoing Irish War of Independence.

Johnny's brother Paddy survived the Civil War and took over the brush-making business where he employed Joe Kenny, his sister Kate's son. Johnny's son, Patrick (Pearse), also worked for Paddy for some time before emigrating to England. This business was later renamed Thomond Brush Works. It is interesting to note that Paddy, who did not die until 1961, did not prepare a witness statement which the government set about obtaining in the 1950s from Volunteer survivors of the 1913-1921 period. However, it would appear even at that stage, many anti-Treaty supporters were suspicious of the motives behind these statements and thus failed to secure the cooperation of many survivors as most perceived it as a 'Free State' project (11). Indeed, Paddy's son, Terry, informed me that while Paddy was happy to prepare and sign statements for former colleagues for pension applications, he was very reluctant to even talk about incidents to him or his family that occurred during the War of Independence or the Civil War.

My grandmother Kate pictured with her young family in the front garden of her house in St Patrick's Road shortly after moving there from Mungret Street in circa 1928. Back row from left; John (Roger-my father), Michael, Denis. Front row; Patrick (Pearse), Robert (Bertie), Catherine (Kate) and Mary.
(Photograph courtesy of Michelle Mac Sweeney and Eileen McNamara)

My grandmother applied for Johnny's War of Independence Service Medal in June 1943 (12) and received it in October 1943 (13). Two types of medals were issued by the Department of Defence. One had what was known as a Comrac Bar (Comrac was the old Irish word for fighting) which was awarded to persons who rendered active military service during the War of Independence (more than 15,000 medals were awarded in that category). The other medal, without a Bar, was awarded to persons whose service was not deemed active military service, but who were members of Óglaigh na hÉireann (IRA), Fianna Éireann, Cumann na mBan or the Irish Citizen Army (more than 50,000 Medals were awarded in this class) (14). Johnny was awarded, quite surprisingly in my view, the latter medal. The reason for this is not clear, but it may be partly due to the nature of how Kate applied for the medal. In her application, my grandmother simply stated that she was seeking a service medal. There was a formal application form that sought more detailed information, which she does not appear to have completed. I would be strongly of the view that Johnny was well entitled to an active service medal for a number of reasons.

The official Department of Defence description of those entitled to a Service Medal with Comrac Bar is that 'Medals were awarded to persons who were in possession of a Military Service Certificate entitling them to a pension under the Military Service Pensions Acts in respect of the period which ended with the Truce of 11th of July 1921' (15). Johnny obtained a military service certificate stating that he saw active service, and this should have been more than sufficient proof to satisfy the above-mentioned minimum requirement. Furthermore, Military service is defined in part 2, section 5. (1) of the Army Pensions Act 1932 as being;

5.—(1) A person shall for the purposes of this Part of this Act be deemed to have been engaged in military service when, but only when, he was on duty as a member of an organisation to which this Part of this Act applies, or was under arrest as a result of his activities as such member, or being such member was evading capture or pursuit by the armed forces of the British Government or of the Government of Saorstát Éireann or of the Provisional Government or of the Government of Northern Ireland, or being such member <u>was detained in a prison or ship, or an internment camp by or by order of any of the said Governments</u>, and the expression

Family Life

Johnny's War of Independence medal (front and rear view). The combination of the colours chosen for the ribbon was adopted by reason of its association with the terms 'Black and Tan'.

The two types of the 1919-1921 War of Independence medals together with an original presentation box. The medal to the right has the Comrac bar and the other medal without the Comrac bar been active. *(Courtesy Clare Archive)*

"military service" shall, in this Part of this Act, be construed accordingly.

In addition to the above-mentioned Military Service certificate Johnny, clearly by virtue of his documented detainment in at least two different internment camps and his documented membership and position in the IRA, should have more than satisfied the above-mentioned requirement to demonstrate military service.

A copy of the certificate from the Department of Defence which were issued in 2006 to replace lost, stolen or destroyed War of Independence Medals, which I applied for and obtained at that time.

LIST OF REFERENCES

Chapter 1- Early years

1. *Census of Ireland*, 1901, 1911.
2. Oral accounts of Terry Mac Sweeney and Joe Kenny.
3. *Census of Ireland*, 1901, 1911.
4. Kevin Hannon, 'The Irishtown', *Old Limerick Journal*, 10, (Spring 1982), p. 6.
5. Oral accounts of Terry Mac Sweeney and Joe Kenny
6. Limerick City Council, *Limerick City Development Plan 2010-14* (Limerick, 2010), p.240.
7. *Census of Ireland*, 1901.
8. Pension application dependant's form dated 15th September 1923
9. *Ibid*.
10. *Census of Ireland*, 1911.
11. Marriage records.
12. Mount St. Lawrence burial records.

Chapter 2- Early Activities

1. *Limerick Leader*, 13 December 1958.
2. Ó'Ceallaigh, Seamus, Murphy, Seán, *One Hundred Years of Glory: A History of Lmerick GAA* (Limerick, 1987), pp. 232, 234.
3. *Limerick Leader*, 13 December 1958.
4. *Limerick Leader*, 9 February 1952.
5. Limerick GAA History Blog. http://limerickgaahistory.blogspot.com/2014/10/young-irelands-gaa-club-limerick-city.html Accessed 27 January 2021.
6. *Limerick Leader*, 13 December 1958.
7. HoganStand.Com http://www.hoganstand.com/laois/MessagePage.aspx?TopicID=934. Accessed 21st. October 2013.

List of References

8. Ó'Ceallaigh and Murphy, *100 Years of Glory*, p. 706; Wikipedia http://en.wikipedia.org/wiki/Limerick_Senior_Hurling_Championship.
9. Ó'Ceallaigh and Murphy, *100 Years of Glory*, p. 235.
10. *Limerick Leader*, 10 November 1912. With thanks to Tom Toomey for highlighting this to me.
11. *Limerick Leader*, 13 December 1958; *Limerick Leader*, 3 April 1911.
12. For example the *Limerick Leader*, April 29 1910 and 10 April 1907.
13. *Limerick Leader,* 7 September 1935.
14. *Limerick Leader,* 13 December 1958.
15. *Limerick Leader,* 29 September 1920 and *Freeman's Journal* 11 April 1923.
16. Back row- J. Gubbins, J. Hayes, F. Murphy, T. O'Brien, J. Mc Namara, J. Creamer.
    Middle row- J. Murphy (Pres), J Fitzgerald, P. Frawley, A. Kelly, M. Halvey, J. Brennan, T. Hayes (Capt.), J. Flanagan (Vice-Captain), J. Mc Sweeney, P O Driscoll, J. Malone (Tres.).
    Front row- T. Mc Mahon, J. Ryan (Sec.), G. Mc Gill, P. Scanlan.
17. Obituary of Paddy Mc Sweeney in *Limerick Leader*, 18 December 1961; BMH, MA Witness statement 1404, Thomas Dargan, p. 1 and BMH, MA Witness statement 1423, Jeremiah Cronin, p. 4
18. *Limerick Leader*, 22 January 1913; 24 March 1913; 20 March 1914.
19. BMH, MA Witness Statement 855, Madge Daly, p.2.
20. *Limerick Leader*, 7 September 1935.
21. Hanley, Brian, *The IRA: A Documentary History* (Dublin, 2010), p. 7.
22. Martin F.X, *The Irish Volunteers 1913-1915: Recollections and Documents* (Dublin, 1963), p. 20.
23. *Limerick Leader*, 26 September 1913.
24. *Limerick Leader*, 16 May 1913.
25. BMH, MA Witness statement 1423, Jeremiah Cronin, pg. 12.

Chapter 3- Formation of the Irish Volunteers in Limerick City

1. Foy, Michael, Barton, Brian, *The Easter Rising* (Sutton, 2004), pp. 7–8.
2. O'Donnell, Ruan, *Limerick's Fighting Story: 1916-1921* (Cork, 2009) edition originally published 1947/49, Mercier Press, Cork, p.31.
3. UCD-archives http://www.ucd.ie/archives/html/collections/irb.html and Martin, *The Irish Volunteers 1913-1915: Recollections and Documents*.
4. Coogan, Tim Pat, *1916: The Irish Rising* (Dublin,1970) p. 33.
5. O'Leary, John, *Recollections of Fenians and Fenianism*, vol I II (London, 1896).
6. BMH, MA Witness Statement 1420, Patrick Whelan, p.2.
7. BMH, MA. Witness Statement 1415, Michael Hartney, P. 4.
8. Corbett, Jim, *Not while I have ammo* (Dublin 2008), p. 36.
9. O'Donnell, *Limerick's Fighting Story*, p. 33.

10. BMH MA Witness statement 1415, Michael Hartney, p..4.
11. Thomas Toomey, *The War of Independence in Limerick 1912-1921* (Dublin, 2010), p. 101.
12. *Ibid.*
13. *ibid* p. 102.
14. BMH, MA Witness Statement 765, James Gubbins, pg. 9.
15. O'Donnell, *Limerick's fighting story 1916-1921*, p. 314.
16. Toomey, *The war of independence in Limerick 1912-1921*, p. 104.
17. O'Donnell, *Limerick's fighting story 1916-1921*, p. 45.
18. BMH, MA. Witness Statement 1324, Joseph Barrett, Pg.6.
19. Kate Kenny's pension application notes and oral account of Joe Kenny.
20. O'Donnell, *Limerick's fighting story 1916-1921*, p. 45.
21. BMH, MA. Witness Statement 525, Michael J. Stack, p.1 and BMH, MA. Witness Statement 1415, Michael Hartney, p.4.
22. BMH, MA. Witness Statement 525, Michael J. Stack, p.1.
23. *Limerick Leader*, 7 September 1935.
24. BMH, MA. Witness Statement 939, Ernest Blyth, p.74.
25. Oral account of Joe Kenny.
26. RTE Archives http://www.rte.ie/archives/exhibitions/1993-easter-1916/2017-survivors/610313-the-survivors-earnn-de-blaghd/ accessed 8 November 2015.
27. O'Donnell, *Limerick's Fighting Story 1916-1921*, p. 313.
28. *Ibid*, p. 314.
29. *Ibid.*
30. *Limerick Leader*, 7 September 1935.
31. BMH, MA. Witness Statement 1423, Jeremiah Cronin, p. 7.
32. O'Donnell, *Limerick's Fighting Story 1916-1921*, p. 313; Martin, *The Irish Volunteers 1913-1915*, pp. 171-179.
33. *Limerick Leader*, 18 December 1961.

Chapter 4 - Events leading up to the Rising of 1916

1 BMH, MA Witness statement 765 James Gubbins, p. 15.
2 *Ibid*, p. 19.
3 For e.g., BMH, MA Witness statement 765 James Gubbins & Witness statement 1420 Patrick Whelan, et al.
4 BMH, MA Witness statement 765 James Gubbins, pp. 20-21.
5 *Ibid*, p. 21.
6 *Ibid.*
7 Coogan, *1916: The Irish Rising*, p. 79.
8 BMH, MA Witness statement 765 James Gubbins, p .21 & 22.
9 Coogan, *1916: The Irish Rising*, p. 79.
10 The Irish Rising Blogspot, http://theirishrising.blogspot.ie/2010_04_01_archive.html accessed 8 November 2013.
11 Coogan, *1916: The Irish Rising*, p. 79.
12 BMH, MA Witness statement 1420 Patrick Whelan, p .10, 11.

List of References

13	BMH, MA Witness statement 765 James Gubbins, p. 25.
14	Oral account of Terry MacSweeney.
15	*Limerick Leader*, 7 September 1935.
16	BMH, MA Witness statement 1420 Patrick Whelan, p. 12.
17	BMH, MA Witness statement 1415 Michael Hartney, p. 4.
18	Military service pension record of Michael Brennan ref 24SP9375 http://mspcsearch.militaryarchives.ie/detail.aspx?parentpriref=#sthash.V15ikVSF.dpuf
19	BMH, MA Witness statement 1068, Michael Brennan, p. 10.
20	*Ibid* p.11 & p.12.
21	BMH MA Witness statement 1415 Michael Hartney, p. 4.
22	*Ibid.*
23	BMH, MA Witness statement 1324, Joseph Barrett, p. 9.
24	Cuimnionn Luinmeac and BMH MA Witness statement 765, James Gubbins, p. 31.
25	BMH, MA Witness statement 1423, Jeremiah Cronin, p.11.
26	Robert Monteith, *Casement's Last Adventure* (Dublin, 1953), p. 193.
27	Monteith, *Casement's Last Adventure*.
28	*Limerick Leader*, 24 March 1913.
29	BMH, MA Witness statement 1700, Alphonsus J. O'Halloran, p. 7.
30	*Ibid* p.12
31	BMH, MA Witness statement 1068, Michael Brennan, p. 6.

Chapter 5- Aftermath of the Rising and before the War of Independence

1	Monteith, *Casement's Last Adventure*, p. 191.
2	*Ibid* p. 199; O'Donnell, *Limerick's Fighting Story 1916-1921*, p .51.
3	BMH, MA Witness statement 0656, Liam Manahan, p. 17.
4	*Freemans Journal*, 11 April 1923; *Irish Examiner*, 12 April 1923.
5	Obituary of Paddy Mc Sweeney in *Limerick Leader*, 18 December 1961.
6	Art O'Donnell Manuscript- Clare County Archives collection.
7	Seán O'Mahony, *Frongoch University of Revolution* (Dublin, 1987), p. 206.
8	BMH MA Witness statement 182, James Wall, p. 4; Sinn Féin Rebellion Handbook, p. 90.
9	O'Mahony, *University of Revolution*, p. 58.
10	*Ibid* pp. 61, 62.
11	*Ibid* p. 75.
12	*Ibid* p. 59.
13	*Ibid* p. 62.
14	*Ibid* pp. 220, 221.
15	BMH, MA Witness statement 1068, Michael Brennan, p. 16.
16	*Ibid* p. 23.
17	British National Archives Kew W035/94/41.
18	*Limerick Leader*, 2 May 1917; *Freemans Journal*, 2 May 1917.

Chapter 6- Activities during the War of Independence

1. BMH MA Witness statement 525, Michael J. Stack, p.3.
2. Obituary in *Limerick Leader*, April 1923.
3. *Ibid.*
4. *Ibid.*
5. Pension application report from Liam Forde dated 28 November 1934.
6. British National Archives Kew ref WO35/139.
7. Oral evidence of my father who informed me that he served as a Captain and on Kate's pension application, the above-mentioned obituary, and A.P.54 service certificate and battalion records.
8. BMH MA Witness statement 1415, Michael Hartney, p.10.
9. *Ibid* p. 5.
10. BMH, MA. Witness Statement 525, Michael J. Stack, pp.1, 2.
11. BMH MA Witness statement 1415, Michael Hartney, p. 4.
12. Toomey, *The War of Independence in Limerick 1912-1921*, p. 41-57.
13. *Ibid* p. 351.
14. O'Donnell, *Limerick's Fighting Story 1916-1921*, p. 323.

Chapter 7- Internment in Wormwood scrubs

1. *Limerick Leader*, 2 February 1920.
2. *Limerick Leader*, 9 February 1920.
3. BMH, MA Witness statement 0186, Thomas J. Doyle, p.15.
4. BMH, MA Witness statement 1415, Joseph Mc Carthy, p. 85.
5. O'Donnell, *Limerick's Fighting Story 1916-1921*, p. 314.
6. BMH, MA Witness statement 1415 Michael Hartney, p.6.
7. Noonan, Gerard, *The eyes of the Irish world are watching': Sinn féin hunger-strikes in Britain, 1920* (Dublin), p. 53.
8. BMH, MA Witness statement 1702, Seán O'Carroll, pp. 15, 16.
9. *Limerick Leader*, 10 May 1920.
10. Pension application.
11. Limerick Leader, 7 May 1920.
12. *Limerick Chronicle*, 30 March 1920; *Limerick Leader*, 29 March 1920.
13. Cork Archive.
14. *Daily Herald*, 30 April 1920.
15. *Daily Telegraph*, 30 April 1920.
16. National archives series ref H0144 piece 1734 ref A7
17. BMH, MA Witness statement 1415 Michael Hartney, p.6.
18. See attached link for names of all internees in photograph http://theirishwar.com/2013/09/ira-hunger-strikers-wormwood-scrubs/ accessed 8 November 2013.
19. *Limerick Leader*, 7 September 1935.
20. Hannigan, D., *Terence MacSwiney: The hunger strike that rocked an empire* (Dublin, 2010).
21. *Limerick Leader*, 13 September 1920.

Chapter 8- Internment in Ballykinlar

1. Liam Ó'Duibhir, *Prisoners of war: Ballykinlar Internment Camp*, p. 39.
2. Pension application form-A.P.4 form 30 June 1924.
3. Ó'Duibhir, *Prisoners of war*, p. 13.
4. Witness statements of others arrested at that time names given in undated press cutting in Daly Papers folder 320.
5. Ó'Duibhir, *Prisoners of War*, p. 281.
6. On my keeping" and in theirs: a record of experiences "on the run", in Derry Gaol, and Ballykinlar Internment Camp" Louise Walsh.
7. Inscription on carved harp (ref to camp 1), notebook in Daly Papers folder 320 confirming hut number and hut photograph.
8. Ó'Duibhir, *Prisoners of War*, p. 13.
9. Undated press cutting in Daly Papers folder 320.
10. BMH MA Witness statement 1322, Art O'Donnell, p. 58.
11. *Ibid* p. 60.
12. BMH MA Witness statement 1322, Art O'Donnell, p. 58 & BMH MA Witness statement 639, Maurice Donegan, p. 7.
13. On my keeping" and in theirs: a record of experiences "on the run", in Derry Gaol, and Ballykinlar Internment Camp" Louise Walsh, p. 42.
14. *Ibid* p. 44.
15. *Ibid* p. 53.
16. BMH MA Witness statement 1415, Michael Hartney, p. 6.
17. Ó'Duibhir, *Prisoners of War*, pp. 197-202
18. BMH MA Witness statement 1322, Art O'Donnell, pp. 62-63.
19. Photograph-
    Back row- Ernest Fowler, Brian Lavey, Thomas Wheatley, James Hennessey, Christopher Mc Cormack.
    Third row- Edward Dee TD, Denis Mc Grath, John Mc Sweeney, John O'Neill, Edward O'Hanrahan, John Halpin, James Mc Kenna, Michael O'Neill.
    Second Row- James Boyle, Michael O'Neill, Paddy Mc Sweeney (mistakenly named Edward on photo), Thomas Kelly, Thomas O'Gorman, Michael Morrissey, Patrick Mc Kenna
    Front row- Joseph Behan, Thomas Dillon, Denis Mc Sweeney, Michael Behan, John Mc Kenna..
20. On my keeping" and in theirs: a record of experiences "on the run", in Derry Gaol, and Ballykinlar Internment Camp" Louise Walsh pp. 77-81.
21. Toomey, The War of Independence in Limerick 1912-1921, p. 52.
22. BMH MA Witness statement 656, Richard O'Connell, p. 22.
23. Pension Records; Dependants Form, 20 September 1923.
24. *The Old Limerick Journal* (Summer 1989), p. 172-174.
25. *New York Times*, 9 December 1921.
    http://query.nytimes.com/gst/abstract.html?res=FB0610FE3A5A1B7A

93C2A81789D95F458285F9 and Kildare Library http://www.kildare.ie/library/ehistory/2013/04/ballykinlar_internment_camp_19.asp accessed 18 November 2013.
26. *Limerick Leader*, 11 December, 1921.

Chapter 9- The Civil War

1. BMH, MA Witness statement 855, Madge Daly, p. 11.
2. *Limerick Leader*, 7 September 1935 p. 10.
3. Ó'Ruaric, Pádraig Óg, *The Battle for Limerick City* (Cork, 2010), p. 37.
4. BMH, MA Witness statement 1068, Michael Brennan, p. 1.
5. Ó'Ruaric, *The Battle for Limerick City*, p. 137.
6. *Ibid*, p. 36.
7. *Ibid*, p. 81.
8. Corbett, Jim, *Not while I have ammo* (Dublin, 2008), p. 85.
9. McMahon, Tony, 'studisque asperrima belli' in *The Old Limerick Journal*, Volume 8 (Autumn 1981), pp. 30-31).
10. Corbett, *Not while I have ammo*, p. 86.
11. Ó'Ruairc, *The Battle for Limerick City*, p. 122.
12. *Ibid*, p. 124.
13. Liam Deasy, *Brother Against Brother* (Cork,1994), p. 65.
14. Ó'Ruairc, *The Battle for Limerick City*, p. 126.
15. In conversation with Des Long.
16. John O'Callaghan, *The Battle for Kilmallock* (Cork, 2011), p. 16.
17. Ó'Ruairc, *The Battle for Limerick City*, p. 127.
18. O'Callaghan, *The Battle for Kilmallock*, p. 65.
19. *Ibid*
20. Pension application form-A.P.4 form 30 June 1924.
21. Pension application report from Michael Colivet, 4 November 1934.
22. Pension application form- A.P. 29 14 November 1927.
23. Pension application report from the Adjutant of the Southern command 19 September 1924 and oral Accounts of Joe Kenny and Terry Mac Sweeney.
24. Pension application report from Liam Forde 28 November 1934.
25. Pension application report from Michael Colivet, 4 November 1934.
26. Daly papers UL, folder 258. Letter to Mayor of Limerick, October 1922; Corbett, *Not While I Have Ammo*, p. 99.
27. National Library (1922). *Limerick Gaol: Report of Eamon Roche T.D. for East Limerick ... prisoner of war treatment ... Mountjoy ... In the prisons.* [S.l.: s.n. National Library of Ireland call no. EPH D549
28. Daly papers UL, folder 258. Letter to Mayor of Limerick, October 1922.
29. On 20 January 1923, two anti-Treaty IRA men were executed at Limerick Jail. Commandant Con McMahon and Volunteer Patrick Hennessy. Daly papers UL, folder 258.

30. National Library; Markiewicz, C. d. (1922). *Challenge: the Republic is seeing inspiriting days ... Limerick Gaol, to the Editor of Freedom ...* [S.l.: s.n.. 1922.
31. Pension application form-A.P.4 form 30 June 1924.
32. *Ibid.*
33. Mahon, Tom, James J. Gillogly, *Decoding the IRA* (Cork, 2008), p. 66.
34. Oral account of Terry Mac Sweeney (Johnny's brother Patrick's son).
35. Pension application report from the Adjutant of the Southern command 19 September 1924.
36. Pension application report from Liam Forde dated 28 November 1934.

Chapter 10- The Republican Plot

1. Des Long, Limerick Republican Plot, Published by Limerick Republican Graves.
2. *Ibid* and *Limerick Leader*, 24 January 1931.
3. Limerick Leader dated 27 March 1927.
4. Limerick Leader dated 19 March, 1934.
5. BMH, MA Witness statement 855, Madge Daly, p. 12.
6. Limerick Leader 7th September 1935 p.10.
7. Age from death certificate submitted with pension application (burial records state 26 and other sources state 25). Account from, pension records, Limerick Fighting story p. 247, Limerick Chronicle 8 March 1921 and 15 March 1921. I have stated that his body was bullet ridden as some sources state that O'Donoghue was found with 8 bullets in his body while others state 18.
8. Age from Limerick Chronicle 08/03/21 and BMH WS0688 Kate O'Callaghan p. 2.
9. Age from burial records. Rank details military records MA/MSPC/RO/134. Account from Irish Republican News, March 16, 2012, and BMH WS 0806 Maire Clancy. Address from *Limerick Chronicle*, 8 March 1921.
10. Age from death cert and burial records. Account from *Limerick Chronicle*, 3 May 1921 and Des Long, *Old Limerick Journal* (Winter 2011), p. 56. Company details from pension records MA/MSPC/RO/134.
11. Age from burial records. Company details from Military Archives MA/MSPC/RO/134. Account from BMH WS 1435 Daniel F. O'Shaughnessy, p. 89; *Tipperary Star*, 26 September 2011.
12. Age and address from burial records. Date of death I have given differs from previous documented source which sated 4 July 1921 as burial records for Henry Clancy (at whose funeral Downey was shot) state he was buried 4 May and burial records for Downey also confirm this date as does Toomey in *War of Independence in Limerick*, g. 54. Account from an article by Long in *Old Limerick Journal* (Winter 2011), p. 57. A Michael Downey from John Street is listed in the Military Archives as a

13. member of the ASU which is most likely the same person.
13. Age from burial records. Account from *Limerick Leader*, 3 April 2012. Military record pension application and Military Archives MA/MSPC/RO/134. Account from *Limerick's Fighting Story*, p. 138, 142.
14. Age from burial records. Account from BMH WS 1435 Daniel F. O'Shaughnessy, p. 89 and *Tipperary Star*, 26 September 2011 and Toomey, *War of Independence in Limerick*, p. 581-583. Company details from Military Archives MA/MSPC/RO/134.
15. Age from burial records. Account from BMH WS 0855 Madge Daly, article by Des Long in *Old Limerick Journal* (Winter 2011), p. 58 and Toomey, *War of Independence in Limerick*, p. 590.
16. Age and date of death from death certificate. Burial records give a date of 19 July and an age of thirty-two. Date of death I have given differs from previous documented source which sated 2 July 1922 as date of death. Another date of death of 19 July is stated in *The Battle for Limerick City*. An account in this book also stated that he was shot dead in action by a Free State sniper in O'Connell Street and not in the City Mills as stated on his pension application, but I have taken the pension application source as being reliable particularly as it is clear he died later on from his wounds. Accounts from *The Battle for Limerick City*, pp. 114, 140 and Official Souvenir, prepared by the West-Limerick Memorial Committee for the unveiling of a Memorial on Easter Sunday, 10 April 1955, by President O'Kelly. Pension record gives the City Mills as the place of his death.
17. Age from burial records. Rank from Military Service Pensions Collection MA/MSPC/RO/134 p. 102 0f 105. Account from *Battle of Kilmallock*, p. 98,99,100 and 139 and *Limerick's Fighting Story*, p. 314. Information about hunger strike from document 1988.0056 Limerick City Museum.
18. Age from burial records. Account from BMH WS 0855, Madge Daly p. 11, BMH WS 1415 Michael Hartney, p. 8 and Michael Hartney's pension application.
19. Age from burial records. Company detail and address from Military Service Pensions MA/MSPC/RO/134 p. 186 of 188. Account from Republican propaganda leaflet published in *Battle of Limerick City*, p. 73, *Battle for Kilmallock*, p. 132 and *Limerick Chronicle*, 8 August 1922.
20. Age from burial records, Company detail and address from Military Service Pensions Collection MA/MSPC/RO/134 p. 186 of 188, although St. Joseph's Street is also mentioned as an address. Account *Battle for Kilmallock*, p. 132; *Limerick Chronicle*, 8 August 1922 and *The War of Independence in Limerick*, p. 326. An E. O'Dwyer of Limerick, listed as killed in action was also listed as a member of the Mid-Limerick Brigade Flying Column MA/MSPC/RO/139.
21. Rank and account from Military Service Pensions Collection File Reference MD18410. Date of death I have given differs from previous

documented source which stated 13 July 1921, death certificate states age and date I have given and also MA/MSPC/RO/134 and burial records also confirm this date but state he was 18 years old. *Limerick Chronicle*, 8 August 1922 states that a Hogan was injured along with the two O'Dwyer brothers and most likely is the same Hogan man mentioned in Republican propaganda leaflet published in *Battle of Limerick City*, p. 73. Account also from pension records.

22. Age and address are taken from the death certificate. Burial records, which tend to be unreliable, state that he was twenty-three. *Limerick Leader* article dated 12 March 1927, states that he was a Volunteer in the Mid-Limerick Brigade, but I have been unable to find a record of him in the Military Service Pensions Collection. However, a document in minute book file of the trustees of the Republican Plot lists him as a member of E-Company. The Account of death and occupation from his family's pension application.

23 Age and date of death from death certificate however burial records state that he was thirty-five and gives the date of death as the twenty-eighth. Company details from Military Archives and account from Republican Graves Committee at http://admin2.fr.yuku.com/topic/9315/Limerick-RepublicanGraves-Committee#.VwO9LrkUW70, *The Battle for Limerick City*, p. 136 and *The War of Independence in Limerick*, pp. 208, 622. Occupation form pension records.

24 Age and place of death, burial records. Address and rank military service pensions collection MA/MSPC/RO/133. Account from *The War of Independence in Limerick*, pp. 319, 353; *The Irish Republican Struggle in Limerick* by Michael Hayes, p. 56 and from the *Limerick War News*, 11 September 1922.

25. BMH WS 0855 Madge Daly p. 2 and Mount Saint Lawrence guidebook.

Chapter 11- Family life

1. Pension application form-A.P.4 form 30 June 1924.
2. Pension application form -dependants form 15 September 1923.
3. Pension application form-AP4 form 30 June 1924.
4. Letters from Department of Defence Army Pension Branch 15 November 1924, 9 January 1928 & A.P. 10 notice, March 1933.
5. Pension records A.P. 25, 6 March 1935.
6. Irish medals.org, http://irishmedals.org/gpage14.html accessed 14 November 2013.
7. Article in *Limerick Leader* circa 1924 with thanks to Tom Toomey for highlighting this.
8. Wikipedia http://en.wikipedia.org/wiki/American_Committee_for_Relief_in_Ireland and http://en.wikipedia.org/wiki/Irish_White_Cross accessed 5 November 2013.

9. Monteith, *Casement's Last Adventure*, p.189.
10. Limerick Leader, 8 April, 1961.
11. Bureau of Military History http://www.bureauofmilitaryhistory.ie/about.html accessed 5 November 2013.
12. Letter to the Department of Defence, 22 June 1943.
13. Pension application records ref. DP.8480.
14. Óglaigh Na Heireann 'Medals of the Irish Defence Forces (1st. Edition)' (2010), p. 94.
15. Irish medals.org, http://irishmedals.org/gpage19.html accessed 14 November 2013.

BIBLIOGRAPHY

Brennan, Michael, *The War in Clare 1911-1921* (Dublin, 1980).

Coogan, Tim Pat, *1916: The Easter Rising* (Dublin, 2005).

Coogan, Tim Pat, *The IRA* (Dublin, 1970).

Corbett, Jim, *Not while I have ammo* (Dublin, 2008).

Deasy, Liam, *Brother against Brother* (Cork, 1994).

Feeney, Brian, *Sean Mac Diarmada-16 Lives* (Dublin, 2014).

Harrington, Michael, *The Munster Republic: The Civil War in North Cork* (Cork, 2009).

Hayes, Michael, *The Irish Republican Struggle in Limerick* (Dublin, 2015).

Hopkinson, Michael, *Green against Green: The Irish Civil War* (Dublin, 1988).

Litton, Helen, *Thomas Clarke-16 Lives* (Dublin, 2014).

Litton, Helen, *Edward Daly-16 Lives* (Dublin, 2013).

Martin, F.X., *The Irish Volunteers 1913-1915: Recollections and Documents* (Dublin, 1963).

Monteith, Robert, *Casement's last Adventure* (Dublin, 1953).

O'Callaghan, John, *The Battle for Kilmallock* (Cork, 2011).

Ó'Ceallaigh, Séamus, *100 Years of Glory, the history of Limerick GAA, 1884-1984* (Limerick, 1987).

O'Donnell, Ruan, (ed), Limerick's fighting story 1916-1921 (Cork, 2009).

Ó'Duibhir, Liam, *Prisoners of War: Ballykinalar Internment Camp* (Cork, 2013).

O'Mahony, Séan, *Frongoch University of Revolution* (Dublin, 1987).

Ó'Ruairc, Pádraig, *The Battle for Limerick City* (Cork, 2010).

Toomey, Thomas, *The War of Independence in Limerick 1912-1921* (Dublin, 2010).

Walsh, Louis J., *On my Keeping and in theirs: a record of experiences on the run, in Derry Gaol, and in Ballykinlar Internment Camp* (Dublin, 1921).

APPENDIX 1

THE FOLLOWING IS A SHORT ACCOUNT OF WHAT BECAME OF JOHNNY'S SIBLINGS

Mary Ellen (Ella)- Was a seamstress and lived in Mungret Street over the brush factory. She had a haberdashery shop at the front of the factory and sold cups, plates, knives, forks, brushes, statues, pots, pans, etc. She never married and went to live with her sister Kate when she got old. She later went into the City Home where she died in the 1950s.

Ann (Nan)- Married Dan Welsh, who joined the British Army and fought in France in World War One, only to become involved in the Volunteers when demobilised. They lived in the first house in Sean Heuston Place beside the old brush-making workshop and had a clothes stall in the market. They had three children.

Kathleen (Sister Elizabeth)	Became a Nun in a convent in Keady, County Armagh and died in 1994.
Christopher (Christy)	Emigrated to England, uncertain whether he returned or died in the UK.
Philomena	Married Tommy McMahon lived in High Street and had a second-hand book shop there which up to recently was run by their son Sean. They moved to O'Callaghan's Mills in later life. Philomena died in the 1980s.

Catherine (Kate)- Married Frederick (Fred) Kenny (mentioned in book and pictured with Johnny in Laffin's Field). He died in 1920 having been shot in the groin in an attack on a barracks and could not get medical help. He subsequently got pneumonia and was taken to St. John's Hospital where he died. Fred, quite interestingly, was born in a building in the Custom House which is now the Hunt Museum. Kate died circa 1948, and they had eight children.

Vincent	Died in a fire in Chicago, USA
Freddy	Died in Dumferlin, Scotland in 1950s.
Anthony (Tony)	Lived in Janesboro, died in the late 1960s.
Joseph (Joe)	Died 1982 (Joe Kenny's father).

Appendix 1

John	Died in Limerick, late 1930s
Angela	Lived in Garryowen, died 1995 (mentioned in the book).
Robert (Bob)	Died in England in the late 1970s
Cornelius (Connie)	Died as a baby in Mungret St.

Denis (Dinny)- Went to Australia and was conscripted into the Australian infantry and fought in France in World War One. Came home to Limerick after the war where and was interned in Ballykinlar. He later emigrated to the USA where he worked as an orderly in a hospital in Long Island, New York. Died in the 1940s and is buried with his nephew Vincent (who was a member of Na Fianna and is mentioned and photographed in the book) in St. Joseph's Cemetery, Central Islip, Long Island, New York.

Patrick (Paddy)- His story is well documented in my research. Paddy married Rebecca (Beck) Moloney from St Mary's Parish, who as mentioned, was active in Cumann na mBan and lived in Sir Harry's Mall (the Sand Mall), and they had five children.

Johnny	Deceased 1990
Vera	Deceased 1949
Ann	Deceased 2004
Terence (Terry)	Christian Brother (ex-CBS Sexton Street), currently residing in Dublin.
Denis	Lived in New Cross, London. Deceased 2017

Thanks to Joe Kenny for providing the above details

INDEX

Ancient Order of Hibernians (AOH) 18
Anglo-Irish Treaty (1921) 28, 49, 73, 85-6, 91-3, 100, 118, 124, 127-8
Asgard 16
Aud 20, 22, 34, 36, 38-9, 43, 54

Ballykinlar Internment Camp 47, 72-90
    Book of Ballykinlar 87
    opening 72
    railway station 74
    Republican prisoners released 86-7
    reputation 73
Banna Strand 34, 36, 37
Benson's Lane 1, 5
Black and Tans 58, 59, 82, 85, 106, 115
Bloody Sunday 1920 49, 72
Blythe, Ernest 26, 28
Boer War 21
Brennan, Michael 40, 43, 50, 92-3
Brixton Prison 62, 70
brush making 1, 2-3, 4-5, 52, 124, 127, 128
Byrne, Tom 62

Cairo Gang 49, 72
Casement, Roger 12, 20-2, 34, 36-7, 44-5, 113
Castleconnell Battalion 35
'Cat and Mouse Act' 51
Ceannt, Eamonn 19
City Battalion 26, 30, 33, 35, 38, 39, 42, 47, 54
Civil War (Irish) 17, 32, 58, 91-105
Clancy, Seoirse 19, 22, 106, 114
Clarke, Thomas 12, 18, 20-1, 44-5
Colbert, Con 12, 44
Colivet, M.P. 26, 35, 38, 100, 102

Collins, Michael 36, 48-9, 85
Connolly, James 19
Cork Prison 54, 73, 74
Croke Park 7, 72
Cronin, Jeremiah 30, 43
Cruises Hotel 94
Cumann na mBan 30, 32, 102, 109, 114, 120, 124, 130, 148

Dáil Éireann 91-2
Daly, Agnes 38
Daly, John 13, 19-20, 21, 32, 44-5, 52, 55, 70
Daly, Madge 91, 103, 106, 107-9, 120
Daly, Ned 20, 44-5
Defence of the Realm Act 32, 60, 64
Dublin Castle 72
Dunne, Peter 62
Dunne, Seamus 62

East-Clare Brigade 92
East-Limerick Brigade 28, 85, 117
executions 12, 19, 20, 21, 44, 45, 103, 107, 114, 115, 118

Ford, Liam 40, 55, 102, 105
Four Courts 20, 92, 93
Frongoch Internment Camp 41, 46-9, 50, 51

Gaelic Athletic Association (GAA) 8, 9, 17, 113, 120, 127
Gaelic League 7, 17, 18, 113, 114
Gaelic revival 2, 17
Galtee Battalion 35
General Headquarters (GHQ) 16, 28, 33, 36
Griffith, Arthur 49
Gubbins, James A. 33, 61, 62
Hartney, Margaret 102, 120

Index

Hartney, Michael 61-2, 102, 105, 109, 120
    prison account 68
Hayes, Dr Richard 85
    Irish Film Censor 85
Heuston, Seán 12, 44, 147
Hobson, Bulmer 12
Home Rule 17, 18, 20
hunger strikes 51
    Cork Prison 70
    Wormwood Scrubs 62, 123
Irish Citizen Army 19, 130
Irish Parliamentary Party 17, 18
Irish Republican Brotherhood (IRB) 8, 10, 18-9, 20, 22, 24, 26, 30, 35, 41-2, 44-5, 54, 70, 114, 123
Irish Volunteers 17-32, 113, 123
    first meeting in Limerick 20
    structure in Limerick 26-8
Irish White Cross 127, 128

Keane, Thomas 107, 108, 115, 118
Kilmainham Jail 45, 124
Kilworth Detention Camp 54, 73

Lane, John 40
Limerick
    Castle Barracks 93, 97
    City Home Hospital 57, 104
    Corporation 2, 66
    Cruises Hotel 94, 95
    New Barracks 73, 93, 98, 104, 116
    Ordnance Barracks 93, 94, 96
    prison 41, 54, 57, 73, 93, 102, 104, 124
    Special Military Area 57
    Strand Barracks 93, 96, 97
Lynch, Liam 93, 94, 98, 104
Mac Donagh, Thomas 18, 44
Mackey, Captain Connie 19, 96
MacSwiney, Terence 45, 70
Mallin, Michael 30
Markievicz, Constance 30, 103

Mc Dermott, Seán 12, 44
Mc Inerney, Major James 40
McNeill, Eoin 38, 39, 42
Mc Sweeney (nee Hogan), Catherine 1
Mc Sweeney (nee Walsh), Catherine 2, 129
Mc Sweeney, Denis (brother) 1, 3, 72, 78, 87, 90
Mc Sweeney, John (Johnny)
    Ballykinlar internment 72-90
    childhood 1-6
    collapse at Buttevant 100
    Cornwallis Infirmary 68
    death of 104
    hurling 7-9, 10, 20
    imprisonment in Limerick 102-3
    insurrection debate (1916) 40-2
    joining the Volunteers 20
    Limerick Guardians 10
    release from Ballykinlar 55, 86-7
    Wormwood Scrubs internment 60-71
Mc Sweeney, Patrick (Paddy) 1, 10, 12, 32, 47-8, 57, 72, 87, 93, 104, 107, 128-9
Mac Sweeney, Brother Terry 47, 57, 129
Mid-Clare Brigade 93
Mid-Limerick Brigade 28, 38, 43, 46, 58, 60, 61, 85, 96, 105, 113, 114-5, 116, 117, 118, 119, 120-3
Monteith, Captain Robert 33-4, 36-7, 43
Mount St Lawrence Cemetery 104, 106, 109
Mulcahy, Dick 49
Munster Fair Tavern 96

Na Fianna 10, 12, 16, 30, 44, 148
National Troops 92, 105

O'Callaghan, Michael 21, 106, 108, 113
O'Donnell, Art
O'Dwyer, Bishop Thomas 47
O'Kelly, Seán T. 50
Ó'Murthuile, Seán 40

Pearse, Patrick 4, 12, 18, 20, 21, 22, 38, 39, 40, 42, 44, 45, 128
Pearse, Willie 44, 107, 113
Plunkett, Joseph 18
Prisoners Defence Fund 127

Redmond, John 17, 18
Richmond Barracks 46
Rising, Easter 1916 12, 20, 24, 26, 30, 33-45, 46-52
    Ashbourne 42, 85
    Carnmore 42
    Clarenbridge 42
    Enniscorthy 42
Rosaville 127
Royal Irish Constabulary (RIC) 41, 52, 55, 56, 57, 60, 66, 94, 116

Sheppard, Oliver 106
Sinn Féin 18, 48, 50, 52, 62, 85, 87, 113, 114, 124
Solohead 53

Transport Union Hall 16

Ulster Volunteers 18

Wandsworth Prison 47, 48
War of Independence
    Johnny's role in 17
    martial law 16, 57
Weldon, Anthony 46, 47
West-Limerick Brigade 28, 35, 119
Whelan, Patrick 19, 37-8, 61, 63, 64
Wolfe Tone Club 19
Wormwood Scrubs Prison 37, 54, 58, 60-71
    conditions 61

Young Irelands (hurling club) 7, 8
Young Ireland Society 8

www.ingramcontent.com/pod-product-compliance
Lightning Source LLC
Chambersburg PA
CBHW040415100526
44588CB00022B/2838